W9-DIR-413

Elizabethan England

Titles in the World History Series

Ancient Greece

The Early Middle Ages

The Late Middle Ages

The Relocation of the North American Indian

The Roman Empire

The Roman Republic

Elizabethan England

William W. Lace

LUCENT BOOKS

An imprint of Thomson Gale, a part of The Thomson Corporation

Detroit • New York • San Francisco • San Diego • New Haven, Conn. • Waterville, Maine • London • Munich

For more information, contact
Lucent Books
27500 Drake Rd.
Farmington Hills, MI 48331-3535
Or you can visit our Internet site at http://www.gale.com

LIBRARY OF CONGRESS CATALOGING-IN-PUBLICATION DATA

Lace, William W.
Elizabethan England / by William W. Lace.
p. cm. — (World history series)
Includes bibliographical references and index.
ISBN 1-59018-655-9 (alk. paper)
1. Great Britain—History—Elizabeth, 1558–1603—Juvenile literature. 2. England—Social life and customs—16th century—Juvenile literature. I. Title. II. Series.
DA355.L333 2005
942.05'5—dc22

2005002100

Printed in the United States of America

Contents

Foreword

Each year, on the first day of school, nearly every history teacher faces the task of explaining why his or her students should study history. Many reasons have been given. One is that lessons exist in the past from which contemporary society can benefit and learn. Another is that exploration of the past allows us to see the origins of our customs, ideas, and institutions. Concepts such as democracy, ethnic conflict, or even things as trivial as fashion or mores, have historical roots.

Reasons such as these impress few students, however. If anything, these explanations seem remote and dull to young minds. Yet history is anything but dull. And therein lies what is perhaps the most compelling reason for studying history: History is filled with great stories. The classic themes of literature and drama—love and sacrifice, hatred and revenge, injustice and betrayal, adversity and overcoming adversity—fill the pages of history books, feeding the imagination as well as any of the great works of fiction do.

The story of the Children's Crusade, for example, is one of the most tragic in history. In 1212 Crusader fever hit Europe. A call went out from the pope that all good Christians should journey to Jerusalem to drive out the hated Muslims and return the city to Christian control. Heeding the call, thousands of children made the journey. Parents bravely allowed many children to go, and entire communities were inspired by the faith of these small Crusaders. Unfortunately, many boarded ships captained by slave traders, who enthusiastically sold the children into slavery as soon as they arrived at their destination. Thousands died from disease, exposure, and starvation on the long march across Europe to the Mediterranean Sea. Others perished at sea.

Another story, from a modern and more familiar place, offers a soul-wrenching view of personal humiliation but also the ability to rise above it. Hatsuye Egami was one of 110,000 Japanese Americans sent to internment camps during World War II. "Since yesterday we Japanese have ceased to be human beings," he wrote in his diary. "We are numbers. We are no longer Egamis, but the number 23324. A tag with that number is on every trunk, suitcase and bag. Tags, also, on our breasts." Despite such dehumanizing treatment, most internees worked hard to control their bitterness. They created workable communities inside the camps and demonstrated again and again their loyalty as Americans.

These are but two of the many stories from history that can be found in the pages of the Lucent Books World History series. All World History titles rely on sound research and verifiable evidence, and all give students a clear sense of time, place, and chronology through maps and timelines as well as text.

All titles include a wide range of authoritative perspectives that demonstrate the complexity of historical interpretation and sharpen the reader's critical thinking skills. Formally documented quotations and annotated bibliographies enable students to locate and evaluate sources, often instantaneously via the Internet, and serve as valuable tools for further research and debate.

Finally, Lucent's World History titles present rousing good stories, featuring vivid primary source quotations drawn from unique, sometimes obscure sources such as diaries, public records, and contemporary chronicles. In this way, the voices of participants and witnesses as well as important biographers and historians bring the study of history to life. As we are caught up in the lives of others, we are reminded that we too are characters in the ongoing human saga, and we are better prepared for our own roles.

Important Dates at the

1533
Elizabeth I is born on September 7.

1536
Michelangelo begins work on his Sistine Chapel masterpiece, The Last Judgment.

1547
Henry VIII dies; Elizabeth's younger half brother, Edward VI, becomes king.

1550
Billiards is played for the first time in Italy.

1557
Influenza epidemic ravages Europe.

1559
Elizabeth I is formally crowned queen of England.

1564
The Reign of Terror begins in Russia.

1565
England begins to manufacture pencils.

1567
Two million Indians die of typhoid fever in South America.

1530 | 1540 | 1550 | 1560 | 1570

Time of Elizabeth I

1585
The first colony at Roanoke, Virginia, is established.

1576
Francois Viete introduces decimal fractions.

1589
Forks are used for the first time at French court.

1600
Dutch opticians invent the telescope.

1570 | 1580 | 1590 | 1600 | 1610

1577
Sir Francis Drake embarks on his voyage around the world.

1586
Kabuki theater begins in Japan.

1592
William Shakespeare's first play, Henry VI, *is performed.*

1603
Elizabeth I dies on March 24 at the age of sixty-nine.

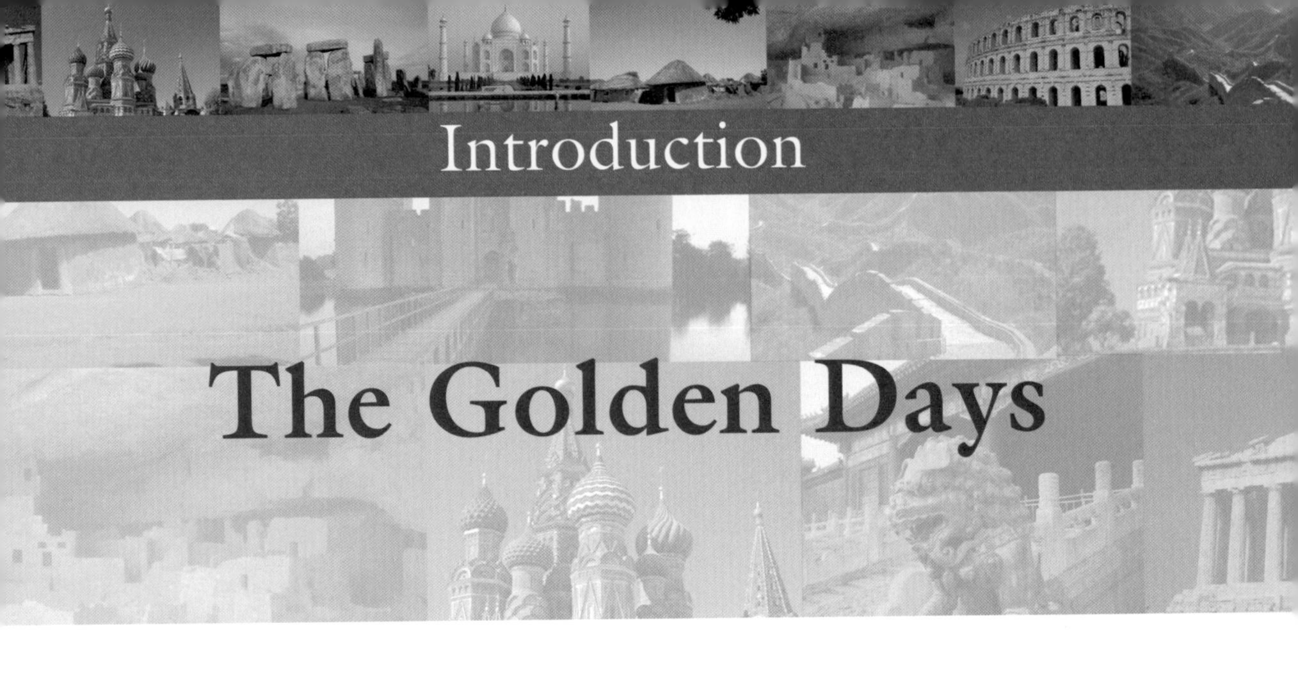

Introduction

The Golden Days

On November 17, 1558, Queen Mary I, the second of King Henry VIII's children to rule England, died. Instead of sorrow, however, her death touched off celebration. Mary's reign had been a national nightmare—defeat in warfare abroad, religious strife at home. England's wealth had been swallowed by war, and its spirit had been exhausted in the bitter struggle between Roman Catholics and Protestants, those who sought to keep their church free from Rome.

Now, the English, except for the Catholic minority, celebrated what they hoped would be a new age of peace, freedom, and prosperity. They rested these hopes on a twenty-five-year-old woman—Elizabeth Tudor, Mary's younger half sister and the last living child of Henry VIII. A week later, as Elizabeth I rode toward London, the people went out to meet her, wrote observer John Hayward, "with so lively representations of love, joy, and hope that it far exceeded her expectations."[1]

Elizabeth's reign was to exceed their wildest dreams. She would rule for forty-five years over what would forever be known as the Elizabethan Age. England would become a respected power in Europe and would expand overseas. Her people would become wealthy. The arts would flourish. Law and government would continue to develop toward a form that eventually would spread throughout the world.

Force of Personality

Elizabeth cannot be given full credit for the accomplishments of Elizabethan England. She was careful, cautious, and conservative. Some achievements during her reign occurred despite her wishes, not because of them. Nevertheless, she gave much more than her name to her reign. It was her

This portrait depicts Queen Elizabeth I of England in her coronation robes, holding a scepter and an orb, the symbols of royal office.

personality—joyous, confident, and defiant—that served as an example to her people and gave them a patriotism never felt before. The people loved Elizabeth, and that love inspired them. Historian A.H. Dodd writes, "The whole age is colored by the rich personality of the Queen herself, but never swamped by it: one of her triumphs was the active response she drew from a wide range of social levels and geographical areas, making her reign equally an age of the ordinary Englishmen."[2]

Long after Elizabeth's death, her reign would be remembered as England's golden age. Indeed, November 17 was celebrated as a national holiday for almost two hundred years. Even while she ruled, her subjects knew they were living in a special time. They called her "Gloriana" because of the glory she had brought to the country. A song of the period went:

> But whereto shall we bend our lays
> [songs]?
> Even up to Heaven, again to raise
> The Maid which, thence descended,
> Hath brought again the golden days
> And all the world amended.[3]

Chapter One

Gloriana and Her Reign

When Elizabeth was told that Mary was dead and that she was now queen, she quoted, in Latin, a verse from the Book of Psalms: "This is the Lord's doing, and it is marvelous in our eyes."[4] It must, indeed, have seemed a miracle to her.

That her family occupied the throne of England was, in itself, highly improbable. Her grandfather, Henry VII, had emerged as king in 1485 from the Wars of the Roses that had decimated the royal houses of Lancaster and York. Henry's claim to royalty was slim at best, resting on the fact that he was the great-great-grandson of King Edward III through his grandmother, whose father had been born illegitimate.

Much of the reign of Elizabeth's father, Henry VIII, was complicated by the lack of a male heir. His first wife, the Spanish princess Catherine of Aragon, gave birth to a daughter, Mary, in 1516, but it eventually became clear that she would bear no more children. Meanwhile, Henry had fallen in love with Anne Boleyn, a young woman at court. He tried to make her his mistress, but she refused him, insisting on marriage. The love-struck king agreed, and in 1527 he set out to have his marriage to Catherine annulled over her bitter objections.

The only person who could annul the marriage of the king of England and a princess of Spain was Pope Clement VII, head of the Roman Catholic Church. Catherine, however, was the aunt of the powerful Holy Roman Emperor Charles V, whom the pope dared not antagonize.

The New Church

For almost six years Henry pulled every diplomatic string possible but was unable to obtain an annulment. Finally his chief adviser, Thomas Cromwell, found a solution. Henry would proclaim a Church of England, separate from Rome, with himself at the head.

In April 1533 Parliament, England's legislative body, passed the Act of Restraint

King Henry VIII (left) had his marriage to Catherine of Aragon annulled so he could wed Anne Boleyn (right), Elizabeth's mother.

of Appeals, severing all ties with the Roman Catholic Church. A month later Archbishop of Canterbury Thomas Crammer, now the highest-ranking clergyman in the country, obligingly declared Henry's marriage to Catherine null and void. The pope promptly excommunicated Henry, and an era of bitter hostility between England's Catholics and Protestants began.

Henry had not waited for a decree of annulment. He and Anne Boleyn had been married in a secret ceremony in January. By the time Anne was crowned queen on June 1, she was noticeably pregnant. Her baby was born on the afternoon of September 7, 1533, in the royal palace at Greenwich. To the great disappointment of Henry and Anne, it was a girl.

Henry hid his frustration as best he could. In a ceremony as elaborate as he could make it, the baby girl was christened "the right high, right noble, and right excellent Princess Elizabeth."[5] The next year Parliament passed the Act of Succession, rendering Princess Mary illegitimate and making the new princess heir to the throne.

A New Queen

Still, Henry was determined to have a son, and his roving eye had settled on one of Anne's ladies-in-waiting, Jane Seymour. Cromwell produced evidence—most of it very flimsy—that Anne had committed adultery. She was arrested and sent to the Tower of London. There, on May 19, 1536, she was beheaded. Eleven days later, Henry and Seymour were married. Sixteen months later Henry finally had a son, whom he named Edward.

The baby prince was declared Henry's heir, and Elizabeth was pronounced illegitimate. Rumors spread that she was not even Henry's daughter but rather the daughter of one of Anne's supposed lovers. No one who saw the child, however, could doubt that Henry was her father. She had the same pale skin and red hair and later the same commanding presence and hair-trigger temper.

Elizabeth's childhood, while not exactly happy, certainly was not miserable. King Henry treated her with genuine affection, and she, in turn, cared very much for him, despite whatever she might have known about what he had done to her mother. She spent much of her time with young Edward, whom she loved, and took advantage of the

An Eloquent Defense

In 1549 Princess Elizabeth, then fifteen years old, was accused by Edward Seymour, Lord Protector for the young King Edward VI, of conspiring with Seymour's brother Thomas to seize the throne. To answer the charge and rumors that she was pregnant with Thomas Seymour's child, Elizabeth wrote an eloquent letter in her defense. This excerpt is found in The Private Character of Queen Elizabeth *by Frederick Chamberlin.*

These be the Things which I both declared to Master Tyrwhit [her interrogator], and also whereof my Conscience beareth me Witness, which I would not for all earthly Things offend in any Thing: for I know that I have a Soul to save, as well as other Folks have, wherefore I will above all Things have Respect unto this same. If there be any more Things which I can remember, I will either write it myself, or cause Master Tyrwhit to write it. Master Tyrwhit and others have told me that there goeth rumours Abroad which be greatly both against my Honor and Honestie (which above all other things I esteem), which be these; that I am in the Tower; and with Child by My Lord Admiral [Thomas Seymour]. My Lord, these are shameful Schandlers [scandals], for the which, besides the great Desire I have to see the King's Majestie [Edward VI], I shall most heartily desire your Lordship that I may come to the Court after your first Determination [as oosn as possible]; that I may show myself there as I am. Written in haste, from Hatfield this 28th of January.

superb tutoring of the noted scholar Roger of Ascham. She learned French, Latin, Greek, and Italian and studied history, philosophy, and theology.

Henry VIII died in 1547, and the eleven-year-old Edward became king. Elizabeth lived in the household of Catherine Parr, Henry's sixth and last wife, who treated her with kindness. Edward died in 1553, probably of tuberculosis, and, despite having been declared illegitimate, his half sister Mary became queen. A devout Catholic, she returned England to the Roman church, married the Catholic king Philip II of Spain, and energetically persecuted Protestants. However, because Protestantism had taken firm hold in England, Mary and her marriage were highly unpopular.

Dangerous Years

These were dangerous years for Elizabeth. Her religious views were distinctly Protestant. Nevertheless, she was careful to conform—outwardly, at least—to her sister's religion. Even so, there were several Protestant plots to remove Mary from the throne and replace her with Elizabeth. Elizabeth doubtless knew of, or at least suspected, these schemes, but she refused to take part in what was a dangerous and perhaps deadly game.

Cautious though she was, Elizabeth could not help getting caught up in the political intrigue of the time. When a rebellion by Sir Thomas Wyatt was crushed, Mary's councillors claimed Elizabeth had supported it. She was arrested and repeatedly questioned. She refused to confess and was sent to the Tower of London. Elizabeth was frantic with fear, afraid that she would share the fate of her mother, Anne Boleyn. She spent two months in the Tower, but her enemies still could find no proof of her guilt. Later, still a prisoner, she was moved to the royal palace at Woodstock.

Elizabeth continued to walk a political tightrope throughout Mary's reign. She gave no encouragement to Protestants who wanted to make her queen. At the same time she skillfully avoided Philip's attempts to marry her off to a foreign Catholic prince. As it became evident that Mary would not have children and that Elizabeth would be the next ruler, more and more nobles gave her their promises of support.

Mary died on November 17, 1558. To the Protestants, who made up the large majority of the English, her death was a deliverance, and Elizabeth was the deliverer. Mary had persecuted Protestants, sending more than three hundred to be burned at the stake, six of them less than a week before her death. People would later sing, "Six days after these were burned to death/God sent us our Elizabeth."[6]

A Warm Welcome

Indeed, it must have seemed to the people of England that dark clouds had given way to brilliant sunshine. As the young queen rode into London on November 28, cheering crowds lined the streets. When the procession reached the Tower of London, where new rulers traditionally stayed until their formal coronation, Elizabeth fell to her knees, saying, "Some have fallen from being princes of this land to prisoners in this place. I am raised from being a prisoner in this place to be a prince of this land."[7]

During the reign of her Catholic half sister, Mary, the young princess Elizabeth (pictured) was imprisoned in the Tower of London for her alleged role in Wyatt's Rebellion of 1554.

What the people saw on that day was a young woman of twenty-five in a cloth of gold dress with an ermine cape about her shoulders. She wore a circlet of gold on her forehead, and her auburn hair, flowing loose in the style of an unmarried woman, framed a pale, oval face. Her resemblance to her father was so strong that at one point along the way a voice shouted, "Remember old King Henry the Eighth."[8] Elizabeth responded with a dazzling smile.

Elizabeth was a born politician. She instinctively knew how to appeal to her people and win their affection. The people loved her, and she loved them in return. Her qualities—beauty, majesty, virtue, wisdom—were revered in her own time by Edmund Spenser in his epic poem *The Faerie Queene,* which gave her a name by which

The Tudor Majesty

The Tudor kings and queens were among the most powerful England has ever known. Historian Christopher Morris sums up their reigns in this passage from his book The Tudors.

"Majesty" was perhaps the quality which the Tudor sovereigns more pre-eminently possessed. The word, however, needs careful definition. It implies that the king is different in kind, not merely in degree, from the most exalted of his subjects; that he is no longer primus inter pares [first among equals], like a feudal overlord; that he lives in a high world of his own, in touch with certain mysteries of state which subjects cannot fully understand. . . . The Tudors very seldom laid their ceremonies by. They made a deliberate cult of the royal 'Progress' and, for all their parsimony [reluctance to spend money], neither Henry VII nor Elizabeth economised on the outward trappings of majesty. A Tudor monarch could be undignified or even frivolous, but none of them would allow the taking of any real liberty, just as a cat may suddenly scratch you in its play if you have gone too far. At the heart of every Tudor sovereign there was something cold, aloof, detached, secretive. . . . No minister, not even [Cardinal] Wolsey [who served Henry VIII] or [Lord] Burghley [who served Elizabeth], can ever have felt certain that he had the royal confidence.

she would be known to her subjects and to history—Gloriana.

Yet Elizabeth had the capacity to seem divine and act very human at the same time. She might rule the people of England, but she was one of them and neither she nor they ever forgot it. One morning, after she had changed her mind repeatedly about leaving for a journey, the frustrated driver of a wagon in the courtyard below her chamber said, "Now I see that the Queen is a woman [just like] my wife."[9] Elizabeth's reaction was typical of her style. She leaned out the window and called the man a villain, but threw some coins to him as well.

The queen took her responsibilities seriously, telling her councillors, "Have a care over my people. . . . See unto them. See unto them, for they are my charge [duty]. I charge you, even as God hath charged me . . . my care is for my people."[10] During the coronation procession, she stood at one point and cried out to the people, "Be ye ensured, that I will be as good unto you as ever queen was to her people. No will in me can lack, neither do I trust shall there lack any power. And persuade yourselves, that for the safety and quietness [peace] of you all, I will not spare, if need be, to spend my blood. God thank you all."[11]

Matters of the Heart

Perhaps no other period in history so completely revolved around the personality of the monarch as did the Elizabethan Age. It was a complex, turbulent time, and Elizabeth was a complex, turbulent person.

She could be cold and cruel. She would fly into rages, boxing the ears of one adviser and throwing her slipper in the face of another, and lashing out, as biographer Carolly Erickson writes, "with words that cut as cruelly as swords."[12] However, as her godson Sir John Harington noted, "when she smiled, it was a pure sunshine."[13] She was intelligent and well educated but also was fond of drinking beer, spitting, picking her teeth, and swearing heartily.

She would do almost anything to avoid making a difficult decision. When urged to do one thing or another by her councillors, she would most often do nothing. As she once wrote to King Henry III of France, "I have let time pass, which I generally find helps more than reasoning."[14]

Constantly on display, she was nevertheless the most private of persons. She never confided completely in anyone. She had learned a hard lesson growing up during the reigns of her brother and sister—keep your thoughts to yourself and your mouth shut and you might keep your head on your shoulders.

The immediate question when Elizabeth became queen was that of her marriage. The question in most minds was not *if* she would marry, but *when*. She was expected to produce an heir. Besides, the notion that a woman could rule by herself, without a strong husband, was unheard of.

Elizabeth's first suitor was her dead sister's husband, Philip, now king of Spain, who wanted to maintain the alliance with England. She pretended to be flattered. She protested that she was not worthy. Actually, she had fallen in love with Robert Dudley, Earl of Leicester. Leicester, however, was already married.

Many believed Elizabeth and Leicester were lovers. The scandal reached a climax when, in September 1560, Leicester's wife was found dead at the bottom of a staircase, her neck broken. The official verdict in the death was suicide, but rumors flew that Leicester had his wife murdered.

Queen Mary I is shown with her husband, Philip of Spain. After Mary's death in 1558, Philip courted the new queen Elizabeth.

At first Elizabeth ignored the gossip. Eventually, however, her most trusted councillor, William Cecil, Lord Burghley, convinced her that in marrying Leicester she might gain a husband but lose her throne. Elizabeth came to her senses. She sent Leicester temporarily away from court. While he remained close to her throughout their long lives, there was no chance of marriage.

Actually, Elizabeth was afraid of marriage. Marriage had brought death to her mother, Anne Boleyn, and public ill will toward her sister, Mary. In addition, she had no wish to share any of her power with a husband. "God's death!" she once shouted at Leicester. "I will have here but one mistress and no master."[15] And when Parliament called on her to marry, she replied, "I am already bound to a husband, which is the kingdom of England."[16]

Mary, Queen of Scots

The pressure on Elizabeth to marry and produce an heir was so intense because the person next in line for the throne was Mary, Queen of Scots, a granddaughter of Henry VIII's sister Margaret, who had married King James IV of Scotland. Elizabeth's councillors knew that the devoutly Catholic Mary, should she become queen, would try to return England to Catholicism and perhaps renew the persecutions of Elizabeth's predecessor.

Catholics in England and throughout Europe tried their best to bring this about.

Elizabeth and Dudley

Robert Dudley, Earl of Leicester, was probably the only man with whom Queen Elizabeth I was ever passionately in love. An ambassador from Scotland, Sir James Melville, recorded a rare glimpse of the queen's deep feelings for Leicester. Melville's description is found in Portrait of Elizabeth I, *edited by Roger Pringle:*

I was required to stay [at court] till I should see [Dudley] made Earl of Leicester and Baron of Denbigh; which was done at Westminster with great solemnity, the Queen herself helping to put on his ceremonial [robe], he sitting upon his knees before her with great gravity. But she could not refrain from putting her hand in his neck, smilingly tickling him, the French Ambassador and I standing by. . . .

She took me to her bed-chamber, and opened a little cabinet, wherein were divers little pictures wrapt within paper, and their names written with her own hand upon the papers. Upon the first that she took up was written, "My Lord's Picture". I held up the candle, and pressed to see that picture so named. She appeared loath to let me see it; yet my importunity prevailed for a sight thereof, and [I] found it to be the Earl of Leicester's picture.

Called the Armada Portrait, this painting of Queen Elizabeth commemorates the English navy's triumphant defeat of the Spanish Armada in 1588.

There were repeated plots to murder Elizabeth and replace her with Mary. Mary certainly knew of and secretly approved of these plots, even after she sought Elizabeth's protection, having fled Scotland after involving herself in a plot to murder her husband. Elizabeth kept Mary a near prisoner for eighteen years, but Mary's lack of caution finally caught up with her. Tricked into involving herself in yet another plot, she was reluctantly condemned to death by Elizabeth and beheaded in 1587.

Mary's death opened the way for an invasion of England by Spain. Philip II, even after Elizabeth rejected his offer of marriage, long supported her right to rule, even though he was a Catholic and she a Protestant. He knew that under Mary, Queen of Scots, England would have become an ally of Spain's rival, France, as Mary had been raised in the French court. Now that Mary was dead, a successful invasion would make Philip ruler of England instead of Elizabeth.

Spain and England had long been on a collision course. It was difficult for Philip, as the most powerful, most religious Catholic king in Europe, to stand by while a Protestant kingdom flourished, sometimes as a result of seizure of Spanish ships. After Mary's execution, he began to assemble a mighty fleet, the Armada, designed to sail from Spain, pick up a Spanish army in the Netherlands, and invade England. The Armada, more than 130 ships strong, sailed in May 1588.

War with Spain

Elizabeth had not wanted war. To her, war was a waste of money. Yet when war came, she went in person to rally her soldiers, who would have to defend the country should her navy fail to stop the Armada. Addressing the troops, she said:

> I am come amongst you as you see, at this time, not for my recreation and disport, but being resolved, in the midst and heat of the battle, to live or die amongst you all, and to lay down for my God and for my kingdome and for my people, my honor and my blood, even in the dust. I know I have the body of a weak and feeble woman, but I have the heart and stomach of a king, and of a king of England too and think foul scorn . . . any prince of Europe should dare to invade the borders of my realm.[17]

The soldiers, as it happened, were not needed. The English navy defeated the Spaniards, not in a great battle, but in a series of skirmishes in the English Channel. The Armada was forced to return home by sailing all the way around Scotland and Ireland and lost more than half its ships.

At that point Elizabeth was almost sixty years old and beginning to outlive some of the people closest to her. Leicester died shortly after the victory. Burghley died in 1598, and the queen grew more and more lonely.

Elizabeth gradually became less active and more temperamental, often lashing out at those around her. Still, she could be regal. Addressing Parliament for the last time in November 1601, she said:

> Though God hath raised me high, yet this I count the glory of my crown, that I have reigned with your loves. . . . It is not my desire to live or reign longer than my life and reign shall be for your good. And though you have had, and may have, many mightier and wiser princes sitting in this seat, yet you never had, nor shall have, any that will love you better.[18]

End of the Reign

Elizabeth died on March 24, 1603. She was sixty-nine years old, an age no English monarch before her had reached. She had given much more than her name to her reign. For all her faults—vanity, temper, and deceit—she was exactly what England needed in 1558, someone to steer the country through the treacherous and dangerous decades to a time of prosperity never before known. The English recognized their debt to their queen. An act of Parliament in 1601 said that "no age either hath or can produce the like precedent of so much happiness under any prince's reign."[19] Nothing, however, expressed what the English felt for Elizabeth more than the scribblings of a schoolboy, John Slye, who wrote in the margin of a book in 1589, "The rose is redd, the leves are grene./God save Elizabeth, our noble Quene."[20]

Chapter Two

The Queen Bee and Her Hive

The focal point of Elizabethan England, the royal court, was like a solar system, planets orbiting a sun. Like some planets, a few members of the court loomed large; others were lesser bodies. Some had satellites of their own. Everything, however, revolved around one sun—the queen. Members of the court shined, but only in reflecting her light.

There was no question who was the focal point, and those who forgot that fact were swiftly reminded. Once, when the Countess of Leicester came to court dressed as extravagantly as Elizabeth herself, the queen boxed her ears, declaring "that as there was one sun that lighted the earth, so there should be one at Court."[21]

The royal court had been a fixture in England for five hundred years. It was introduced by William the Conqueror, the French duke who successfully invaded the island in 1066, defeating the Anglo-Saxon inhabitants. At first, the members of the court dealt exclusively with military and administrative matters. They also helped the king administer justice, a function eventually assumed by separate courts of law.

As the gulf in status between king and nobles increased, the court grew larger and began to take on household duties as well. For example, the chamberlain supervised the king's personal quarters. The chancellor served as his public and private secretary. The steward saw that the entire household was properly run. Members of the nobility were honored to hold such titles, although others did the actual day-to-day work.

Perceptions of Power

Still, the English royal court was far from the elegant center of culture it would become under Elizabeth. Her grandfather, Henry VII, was able to see that the appearance of wealth and power was almost as important as wealth and power themselves. As a result, the English royal court grew both in size and splendor. Henry copied the fashions of France and surrounded himself with pomp and ceremony, rich furnishings, and costly apparel. He did not much care for such magnificence personally, but knew he had to project a strong image.

Henry VIII, Henry's son, established an even grander court, and Elizabeth carried on in their tradition. Consequently, her court became a magnet, attracting the best and worst of society. The most talented musicians, the most gifted playwrights, the most able administrators, the most dashing men, and the most beautiful women vied with one another for places close to Elizabeth. Yet because court was the origin of all wealth and power, it was also a place where treachery, jealousy, and scandal abounded.

Ambitious sons and daughters of noble families throughout the kingdom came to court to seek their fortunes. Obtaining a place at court, however, was not easy. There were many job seekers and few jobs. Only

Courtiers carry Queen Elizabeth in a litter during a procession. The pomp of such processions impressed Elizabeth's subjects and foreign observers alike.

A Royal Procession

Paul Hentzer, a German visitor, watched Queen Elizabeth I and her attendants process through the halls of Greenwich Palace on a Sunday morning in 1598. He wrote a famous account of the sight, which is found in Gloriana's Glass, *edited by Alan Glover:*

First went the gentlemen, barons, earls, knights of the garter, all richly dressed and bareheaded; next came the chancellor, bearing the seals in a red-silk purse, between two; one of which carried the royal scepter, the other the sword of state, in a red scabbard, studded with golden fleurs de lis [the French symbol of royalty], the point upwards: next came the queen, in the sixty-fifth year of her age, as we were told, very majestic; her face oblong, fair, but wrinkled; her eyes small, yet black and pleasant, her nose a little hooked, her lips narrow, and her teeth black: (a defect the English seem subject to, from their too great use of sugar); she had in her ears two pearls, with very rich drops; she wore false hair, and that red; upon her head she had a small crown reported to be made of some of the gold of the celebrated Lunebourg table. . . . As she went along in all this state and magnificence, she spoke very graciously, first to one, then to another, whether foreign ministers, or those who attended her for different reasons, in English, French, and Italian. . . . The ladies of the court followed next to her, very handsome and well shaped, and for the most part dressed in white; she was guarded on each side by the gentlemen pensioners, fifty in number, with gilt battleaxes.

those from the highest-ranking and most powerful families could be assured of a position.

If one did not have the right pedigree, another method of securing a position was to flatter Elizabeth, who never tired of people praising her wisdom, dancing, learning, and—most of all—her beauty. She shamelessly fished for compliments and seldom failed to catch them. Elizabeth was usually wise enough, however, to see the purpose behind the fair words.

Court Offices

Those who were not close enough to the queen to employ flattery might employ someone closer to put in a good word for them. There was always a chance of catching the eye of a Burghley or a Leicester, who might give them a position directly or bring them to the attention of the queen, who might appoint them to an office. These offices—"clerk of the wardrobe," for instance—sounded humble but were considered positions of honor and were held by members of the upper classes. The actual work was done by servants.

Others who had or could find no court connections had to buy their way in. Even to get an interview, a newcomer often had to offer a gift, actually a bribe, to someone who could provide an introduction to the queen and her leading ministers. One father spent more than £1,300—enough to buy several good-sized farms—to make his daughter a maid of honor.

Under Elizabeth's father and grandfather, men often served in dual roles both as personal attendants to the monarch and in offices of state. When a queen ruled, however, administrative duties went to men, and household service, for the most part, to women.

The women who served Elizabeth did so at four levels—ladies of the bedchamber, gentlewomen of the privy chamber, maids of honor, and chamberers. The ladies of the bedchamber, usually four in number, were the queen's closest friends. Catherine Ashley, who had been appointed Elizabeth's governess when she was four years old, was among the first group. So was Blanche Parry, who had been in the queen's household even longer, as well as Elizabeth's first cousin Catherine Knollys, daughter of Anne Boleyn's sister Mary.

The Gentlewomen

The gentlewomen of the privy chamber ranked next. These eight women were also of noble birth but were usually not as intimate with the queen as the ladies of the bedchamber. Some had specific duties, such as "the keeper of the plate," *plate* meaning not only dishes but also other forms of precious metal. Others appeared to have no responsibilities but to wait on the queen.

Most of the responsibility for running the household fell on the four chamberers. They were usually not from the nobility but were chosen for their ability to direct the work of the servants. Their duties included storing linen, plate, and a wide variety of other household items.

The six to eight maids of honor were more ornamental than functional. They were young, beautiful, unmarried, and were drawn from the noblest families of England. They accompanied the queen almost everywhere she went. Arrayed beside and behind Elizabeth as she held court, they acted as a backdrop against which she displayed herself to best advantage.

If a maid of honor served Elizabeth faithfully, she could look forward to an arranged marriage of wealth and prestige. She risked losing everything, however, if she married without the queen's permission or—worse yet—became pregnant out of wedlock.

Elizabeth Throckmorton was one of the fortunate maids of honor. Her brother went to considerable trouble and expense to obtain a position for her close to the queen. She served well and wound up marrying Sir Walter Raleigh, one of the queen's favorites. Not as lucky was Mary Fitton. In 1601 Robert Cecil wrote about "a misfortune befallen Mistress Fitton, for she is proved with child, and the Earl of Pembroke, being examined, confesseth a fact, but utterly renounceth all marriage. I fear they will both dwell in the Tower awhile, for the Queen had vowed to send them thither."[22]

Men of the Court

There were fewer men on the staff. The gentlemen of the privy chamber ranked highest, and only two men were to hold this post—John Ashley, husband of Catherine Ashley, and Sir Christopher Hatton. They had no definable duties but were expected to be on call when needed by the queen. When she needed more than one or two male attendants, there were a number of unpaid courtiers available who were always eager for a chance to make an impression on the queen.

There also were six grooms of the privy chamber, either trusted attendants from Elizabeth's previous households or bright

Two robed gentlemen of the court stand near a royal guard, waiting to hold audience with Queen Elizabeth.

young men from good families. The other privy chamber office was that of the gentleman usher. This official was very important to Elizabeth because he controlled who could enter the presence chamber. She trusted him to keep out those in her disfavor or anyone she did not want to see for some reason. Many more positions dealt with matters beyond the privy chamber, and some were among the most important at court. The lord chamberlain had the overall responsibility of running the entire household, not just that of the queen. The lord chamberlain had considerable power because he determined who could and could not live at court. He also was in charge of all entertainments, although these were actually arranged by another officer, the master of revels. Other high-ranking posts, some of which carried only ceremonial duties, included the master of horse, lord steward, chief butler, captain of the guard, and treasurer of the chamber.

Outstanding beauty was not necessarily a desirable attribute for aspiring maids of honor, as Elizabeth was careful not to surround herself with women far more attractive than herself. For men, however, physical attractiveness, elegant clothes, and polished manners were often the best ways to attract Elizabeth's attention.

Looking the Part

A successful courtier had to look the part, and one of the most distinctive aspects of the Elizabethan Age was the extreme, sometimes bizarre, manner of dress. A seventeenth-century historian, William Camden, wrote:

> In these days a wondrous excess of apparel had spread itself all over England [which] grew into such contempt, that men by their new fangled garments, and too gaudy apparel, discovered a certain deformity and arrogancy of mind whilst they jetted up

A courtier sitting for a portrait models the stylish ruff that was so popular in Elizabethan fashion.

Making a Goodly Show

Appearances were everything at Elizabeth's court, and it was not unusual for people to try to get attention by spending everything they had on clothes. William Harrison had the following impression of court dress in his Description of England. *The passage is found in* The Horizon Book of the Elizabethan World *by Lacey Baldwin Smith, edited by Norman Kotler.*

How curious, how nice [finicky] also, are a number of men and women, and how hardly can the tailor please them in making it fit for their bodies! How many times must it be sent back again to him that made it! What chafing, what fretting, what reproachful language doth the poor workman bear away! And many times when he doth nothing to it at all, yet when it is brought home again it is very fit and handsome; then must we put it on, then must the long seams of our hose be set by a plumb line; then we puff, then we blow, and finally sweat till we drop, that our clothes may stand well upon us. . . . Some lusty courtiers also and gentlemen of courage do wear either rings of gold, stones, or pearl in their ears, whereby they imagine the workmanship of God not to be a little amended. but herein they rather disgrace than adorn their persons, as by their niceness in apparel, for which I say most nations do not unjustly deride us, as also for that we . . . bestow most cost upon our arses, and much more than upon all the rest of our bodies, as women do likewise upon their heads and shoulders.

and down in their silks glittering with gold and silver, either embroidered or laced.[23]

The distinctive feature of Elizabethan fashion was the ruff, a construction of starched material that stuck out in a circle around the neck and was held in place with hundreds of sticks. Ruffs were very fragile, and the wearer had to avoid brushing against walls, curtains, other people's ruffs, and—for obvious reasons—candles.

All this, of course, was very expensive. People hoping to make an impression at court frequently spent everything they had on a single outfit and thus, a Spanish observer wrote, "carry their whole estates upon their backs."[24] The most elaborate and costly apparel was that of Elizabeth herself. Every gown was covered with gold and silver braid, pearls, and jewels.

Pomp and Ceremony

Thus clad, the queen and members of the court carried out their day-to-day activities with the utmost pomp and ceremony. The mealtime pageantry, for instance, started with two ushers entering the hall, kneeling three times before the empty table before setting the cloth. Others followed and, after kneeling, placed salt, bread, and plates on the table. Two of the queen's ladies, also after deep curtsies, then rubbed the plates with the bread and salt, tokens of prosperity. Twenty-four guardsmen then carried in the food on golden dishes, after being given a mouthful each to test for poison.

At last, all was ready, but Elizabeth herself was almost never there. Instead, her maids of honor would serve her plate and take it to a private room where she ate, usually from no more than three or four of the dishes. She would appear, however, at state banquets, which might feature as many as three hundred dishes.

The ceremony was equally elaborate each time the queen went out in public. A French ambassador wrote in his report that

> when the Queen goes abroad in public the Lord Chamberlain walks first, being followed by all the nobility who are in Court, and the Knights of the Order [of the Garter] walk after, near the Queen's person. . . . After come the six heralds who bear maces before the Queen. After her march the fifty Gentlemen of the Guard, each carrying a halberd [combination battle-axe and pike], and sumptuously attired; and after that the Maids and Ladies who accompany them very well attired.[25]

Such displays were costly, and Elizabeth bore the expense grudgingly. She was notoriously tight-fisted. She loved, however, for people to spend money on her. She gave all members of the court presents of plate at New Year's, in amounts carefully measured according to the recipient's status. The courtiers, in return, were expected to give the queen presents worth more than what they received. In 1562 these gifts ranged from a silver writing set adorned with pearls from Sir William Cecil to a mince pie from baker John Betts. The total value was £1,262, or about $190,000 in modern terms.

Royal Palaces

Such elaborate ceremonies required equally elaborate stages, and Elizabeth had several at her disposal. The court, physically speaking, was wherever she happened to be. She was not much of a builder of palaces. After all, palaces cost money. Fortunately for her, however, her father and grandfather had constructed or rebuilt many royal residences that were among the finest in Europe, such as Hampton Court, Whitehall, Nonsuch, and Greenwich.

The queen and the approximately fifteen hundred people who made up the court moved among these palaces throughout the year. Such frequent relocation was necessary because of the lack of sanitation at the time. Even though one owner of one Elizabethan manor called his home a "romancy pleasant place,"[26] they were often anything but pleasant. Perfume and incense could never mask the assortment of foul smells that permeated even the royal palaces. These odors were produced by hundreds of pounds of daily kitchen refuse and the large amount of animal and human waste, not to mention the animals and humans themselves. Hundreds of persons lived in cramped quarters. Even the grandest nobles bathed only infrequently, and the servants did not bathe at all. An observer wrote that even the air in the queen's bedchamber was sour.

The fact that many of Elizabeth's principal residences were located on the banks of the Thames River was no help. Even though the river was by far the easiest way to travel, since roads were often rough and muddy, it was where the waste was thrown, not only from the palaces but also from every town along the bank. To protect themselves from the stink of the river, Elizabeth and her courtiers held pomanders to their noses, containers holding perfume or sweet-smelling herbs. Pomanders were also used on a daily basis in the palaces. When one residence became uninhabitable, the court moved on to another while servants remained behind to "sweeten" the former abode.

The Progresses

Elizabeth's desire to show herself to her people, combined with her restless personality, was so intense that moving from palace to palace was not enough. In addition, she spent much of the summer traveling throughout the kingdom on "progresses," the court moving with her. While these journeys were memorable for the common folk who got to see their queen, they took their toll on the courtiers and were very much a mixed blessing for those who played host to the queen. A visit from Elizabeth was an honor, but a very expensive one.

The queen and her court lodged at palaces like Hampton Court for short periods of time, moving frequently for health reasons.

Intrigue at Court

Elizabeth's court was a place where the greatest men in the kingdom vied with one another for the attention and favor of the queen. When she showed favor to one courtier, it was bound to create jealousy in another, as this excerpt from a letter by the Earl of Essex shows. It is found in The Horizon Book of the Elizabethan World *by Lacey Baldwin Smith, edited by Norman Kotler.*

Yesternight the queen came to Worth Hall. . . . She came to speak of [Sir Walter] Raleigh, and it seemed she could not well endure any thing to be spoken against him; and taking hold of one word, 'disdain,' she said there was no such cause why I should disdain him. This speech troubled me so much that as near as I could I described unto her what he had been and what he was, and then I did let her see whether I had cause to disdain his competition of love, or whether I could have comfort to give myself over to the service of a mistress that was in awe of such a man. I spake, what of grief and choler, as much against him as I could, and I think he standing at the door might very well hear the worse that I spoke of himself. In the end I saw she was resolved to defend him, and to cross me. . . . I told her . . . I had no joy to be in any place but loathe to be near about her when I knew my affection so much thrown down, and such a wretch as Raleigh highly esteemed of her. To this she made no answer, but turned away to my lady of Warwick. This strange alteration is by Raleigh's means, and the queen that hath tried all other ways now will see whether she can by these hard courses drive me to be friends with Raleigh, which rather shall drive me to many other extremities.

As one of Elizabeth's favorites, Sir Walter Raleigh (pictured) aroused the enmity of the Earl of Essex, a rival courtier.

Being queen meant never having to ask for permission to pay a visit or wait to be invited. As courtier William Harrison wrote, "Every nobleman's house is her palace, where she continueth during pleasure and till she return again to some of her own."[27] Some tried their best to avoid having Elizabeth as a guest. Some pleaded that their houses were too small or too uncomfortable. That made no difference to the queen, who was sure to get the best quarters, anyway. The bishop of Winchester found that even claiming that plague was in a nearby village failed to dissuade her from visiting him.

People receiving Elizabeth as a guest went to great pains to outdo one another in the lavishness of their welcomes. She could count on hearing one, and usually many more, elaborate orations extolling her beauty, wisdom, majesty, and any other virtue that came to mind. At Cowdray, the home of Lord Montague, a gatekeeper turned orator hailed her as "the wisest, fairest and most fortunate of all creatures. . . . O Miracle of Time! Nature's Glory! Fortune's Empress! The World's Wonder!"[28]

Elizabeth never grew tired of hearing her beauty, wisdom, courage, or any other virtue praised. She delighted in keeping suitors and admirers in constant attendance. As she grew older and tried to maintain a youthful appearance with wigs and makeup, the flattery grew more extreme.

Endless Flirtations

Elizabeth was a shameless flirt. She pretended to be angry but was secretly delighted when men came to blows or fought duels over her. It was all very charming when she was young, but, as modern historian Christopher Morris notes, later the court was marked by "an often coarse frivolity, by a false hilarity . . . or by the elaborate make-believe of flirtation which had to be kept up long after it had lost all point or savour. It was all frankly vulgar."[29] Even one of the queen's favorites, Sir Walter Raleigh, became bitter and wrote, "Go tell the court it glows and shines like rotten wood."[30] The Elizabethan court may have been gaudy and extravagant, but it also fostered much intellectual and cultural development. The best in music, art, drama, and literature was found at court. Foreign influence was considerable, with some of the most talented persons in France, Italy, and the Netherlands working in London. Their presence, in turn, influenced English writers and artists. The importance of Elizabeth's court, then, is not the glittering picture it presented but rather the fact that it, as historian A.L. Rowse writes, "was the effective point of contact with the Renaissance influences from abroad."[31]

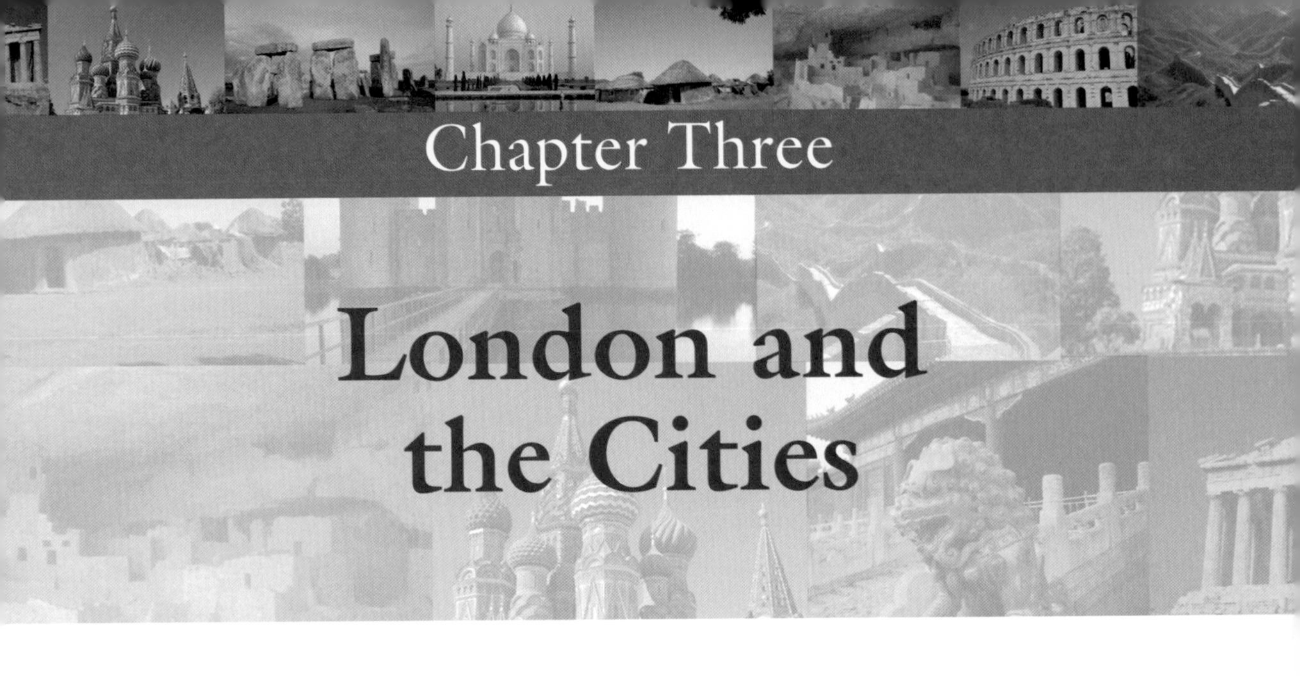

Chapter Three

London and the Cities

England in the Elizabethan Age was more peaceful and prosperous than it had been for more than a century. Trade flourished, and the centers of trade were the cities. The period featured a marked growth of cities, not only in size but also in importance.

In previous centuries, the large manor farms of the nobility formed the center of the English economy. These farms were largely self-sufficient; almost everything the people needed was grown or made on the premises. Towns provided markets, places where people from the farms could bring goods to trade for what they could not produce.

The towns grew during the Tudor era because of changes in the economy. First, agriculture became more specialized. Farms grew the crops or raised the livestock best suited to the land instead of trying to produce a little of everything. This meant a great increase in the buying and selling of farm products among various parts of the country and thus a great increase in the size of market towns.

Second, under the Tudors the basis of the English economy began to shift from raw materials to the manufacture of finished goods. The English were tired of paying high prices to other countries for goods that had been made from raw materials from England. Leather goods were made in Leicester using hides from surrounding cattle farms—hides that had previously been sold overseas. Instead of exporting raw wool, farmers around Norwich sold it to weavers in the town, who produced finished cloth. Instead of being shipped to Europe, iron ore went to cities like Sheffield, which soon became famous for its knives and tools. This manufacturing was centered in the towns and cities, thus increasing their populations.

Manufacturing and Merchants

Manufacturing was done on a small scale—in households or small shops instead of in

Elizabethan England

Hampton Court Palace
One of several palaces occupied by Queen Elizabeth and her court

Tower of London
The queen's enemies were imprisoned and sometimes executed here

Westminster Abbey
Cathedral where Queen Mary and Queen Elizabeth are buried

SCOTLAND
North Sea
North Channel
Atlantic Ocean
IRELAND
Irish Sea
York
Sheffield
Lincoln
Chester
Leicester
Norwich
Cambridge
ENGLAND
WALES
Oxford
London
Reading
Thames River
Dover
Winchester
Southampton
Portsmouth
Plymouth
Strait of Dover
English Channel
FRANCE

This painting shows London as it looked close to the end of Elizabeth's reign. London Bridge, St. Paul's Cathedral, and the Tower of London can all be seen.

large factories—and a metalsmith in Sheffield, for instance, was not able to handle overseas sales himself. This function was performed by a merchant who would buy goods from several manufacturers and then arrange for their export and sale. The growth of trade during Elizabeth's reign and the movement toward a money economy (selling goods for cash instead of trading them for other goods) led to growth in the number and wealth of merchants. "Never in the annals of the modern world," writes modern economist John Maynard Keynes, "has there existed so prolonged and so rich an opportunity for the business man."[32] It was the merchants, and the amount of wealth they controlled, who gave the cities economic power.

In Henry VIII's time, England had a total population of about 3 million, of which some two hundred thousand lived in towns and cities. By the end of Elizabeth's reign, the total population had climbed to 5 million and the number in cities to 1 million.

London was supreme in both size and influence. At the end of Elizabeth's reign, it was the largest city in northern Europe, with a population estimated at three hundred thousand—seventeen times its nearest rival, Norwich. More than 90 percent of the country's overseas trade was done from London. London's importance, as a modern historian writes, "surpassed that of all the rest of the leading towns together."[33]

Despite its population, London was nowhere near the sprawling metropolis it is today. Most of the people were crowded into and around the area bounded by the ancient city walls and the Thames River, containing the Tower of London and St. Paul's Cathedral. Open fields lay between London and Westminster, the center of government. Chelsea and other areas now considered the heart of the city were then simple country villages.

Problems of Growth

The rapid growth of London created problems of housing, food, and water. Housing was built on every available piece of land, including those formerly occupied by Roman Catholic monasteries. Much of the new areas were, as contemporary historian John Stow writes, "inclosed about or pestered with small tenements and homely cottages, having inhabitants . . . more in number than in some cities in England."[34]

Indeed, the crowding was so intense that London finally burst its medieval bounds, expanding outside the ancient walls. Westward expansion was very different from that to the east. As the seaport grew eastward toward Greenwich, it was accompanied, according to Stow, by "a continual street, or filthy straight passage, with alleys of small tenements or cottages . . . inhabited by sailors and victuallers."[35]

London grew in power as well as size. It was governed almost independently of the queen and her council. The merchants in London and the queen's ministers in Westminster were highly respectful of and needed one another. The royal government would have been hard-pressed to pay its bills without the taxes paid by the merchants. At the same time, the government passed laws—such as those placing taxes on imported goods—that guaranteed more profits for the merchants so that they could continue to pay taxes.

Elizabeth was eager to please the London merchants. In 1580, for instance, the London council became concerned with the rapidly increasing population of the city's suburbs, over which they had no control. They asked Elizabeth to help them limit suburban growth. The queen accommodated them by proclaiming that no new houses should be built within 3 miles (4.8km) of the city unless there had previously been a house on the same spot.

London and Paris Compared

A very prejudiced Thomas Gainsford, in his The Glory of England, *gave this comparison of the capital cities of England and France. It is found in* The Horizon Book of the Elizabethan World *by Lacey Baldwin Smith, edited by Norman Kotler.*

Instead of a beastly town and dirty streets [in Paris], you have in London those that be fair, beautiful, and cleanly kept; instead of foggy mists and clouds, ill air, flat situation, miry springs, and a kind of staining clay, you have in London a sun-shining and serene element for the most part, a wholesome dwelling, stately ascension, and delicate prospect; instead of a shallow, narrow, and sometimes dangerous river, bringing only barges and boats with wood, coal, turf, and south country provision, you have at London a river flowing twenty foot, and full of stately ships that fly to us with merchandise from all the ports of the world, the sight yielding astonishment, and the use perpetual comfort.

In this contemporary painting, the Court of Wards and Liveries meets under the direction of Lord Burghley, Master of the Court.

The Livery Companies

London's most powerful forces were the twelve livery companies, groups of merchants that had evolved from the medieval guilds—craftsmen banded together to advance and control their professions. There were companies for drapers, grocers, fishmongers, tailors, and mercers (textile dealers), among others. The city's governing council was made up of aldermen, one elected from each of London's twenty-four boroughs (sections). The aldermen, almost all members of the livery companies, selected the Lord Mayor. Even today, the City of London's aldermen must select the Lord Mayor from two candidates proposed by the livery companies.

The companies strictly controlled who would enter their respective professions, the standards of workmanship, and prices. One could not sell fish, for instance, if he were not a member of the fishmongers company. One joined a company first as an apprentice, serving under a member of the company, and worked his way up to becoming a "freeman," or full member.

London was full of apprentices. They had left their families and lived with their masters. Although the masters sought to control their behavior, these young men were known for drinking and carousing.

By today's standards, London was almost an unlivable city. The streets were crooked, narrow, and filthy. John Stow, who wrote a description of London at the time, said that one street, Chick Lane, was known by most people as "Stinking Lane." People simply dumped their garbage in the street or in the kennels where they kept their dogs. In 1563 the people living near Finbury Court put their garbage, including human and animal excrement, into a pile that grew so large that the council of aldermen had to order "the filthy dunghill lying in the highway near unto Finbury Court be removed and carried away."[36]

The Vermin Problem

As a result, rats and other vermin abounded. Laws called for each person to keep his or her property clean, but these were largely ignored, except when the plague struck. Then city authorities made sure garbage was burned. At other times, people hired the rat catcher, who went from street to street singing:

> Rats or mice, ha' ye any rats or mice,
> polecats or weasels,
> Or ha' ye any old sows sick of the
> measles?
> I can kill them, and I can kill moles,
> And I can kill vermin that creepeth up
> and creepeth down, and peepeth
> into holes.[37]

The Plague

Crowded cities in Elizabethan England were breeding grounds for diseases, the deadliest of which was the plague, here described by Thomas Dekker in his Worke for Armourer's. *It is quoted in* The Horizon Book of the Elizabethan World *by Lacey Baldwin Smith, edited by Norman Kotler.*

The purple whip of vengeance, the plague, having beaten many thousands of men, women, and children to death, and still marking the people of this city every week by hundreds for the grave, is the only cause that all her inhabitants walk up and down like mourners at some great solemn funeral, the City [London] herself being the chief mourners. The poison of this lingering infection strikes so deep into all men's hearts that their cheeks, like cowardly soldiers, have lost their colors; their eyes, as if they were in debt and durst not look abroad, do scarce peep out of their heads; and their tongues, like physicians ill-paid, give but cold comfort. By the power of their pestilent charms all merry meetings are cut off, all frolic assemblies dissolved, and in their circles are raised up the black, sullen, and dogged spirits of sadness, of melancholy, and so, consequently, of mischief. Mirth is departed and lies dead and buried in men's bosoms; laughter dares not look a man in the face; jests are, like music to the deaf, not regarded; pleasure itself finds now no pleasure by in sighing and bewailing the miseries of the time. For, alack! what string is there now to be played upon whose touch can make us merry?

Most cities had "scavengers," people hired to keep the streets clean not only of garbage but also of horse droppings. The city of Oxford hired a person "to carry all sweepings of men's houses and the dirt that cometh of the sweepings of the streets." Every homeowner paid a certain amount every three months "for the carriage [carrying] of the same, and they that have horses to pay for their dung-carriage as the scavenger and they can agree."[38]

Upper stories of houses were built out over the street, shutting out most sunlight, even in daytime. All people were supposed to hang lanterns outside their houses at night, but these lanterns, made of horn and discolored by smoky candles, gave off very little light. Consequently, robbers lurked in the shadows, ready to pounce on the unlucky passerby. Cautious people, if they had to be out after dark, went in groups or hired guards with torches.

London Crime

Criminals were everywhere, especially in the suburbs like Southwark, on the south side of the Thames. These were outside the control of the city of London and its system of constables and watchmen. Enforcement of the law was lax, and prostitution abounded. The crowded streets swarmed with cutpurses and pickpockets. There were even schools for pickpockets, such as the one described by a man of the period:

> There was a school house set up to learn young boys to cut purses. There were hung up two devices, the one was a pocket, the other was a purse. The pocket had in it certain counters, and was hung about the hawks' bells, and over the top did hang a little sacring bell [a small bell used in a church], and he that could take out a counter without any noise was allowed to be a public foyster [thief], and he that could take a piece of silver out of the purse, without the noise of any of the bells, he was adjudged a judicial nipper [pickpocket].[39]

Crime was less widespread within London itself but was still more than could be controlled by the watchmen. The streets were so crowded that a pickpocket or cutpurse could easily escape. At night, when the streets were less crowded, criminals would escape notice of the watchmen by taking refuge in jails, bribing the jailers to get a place to sleep until morning.

The Thames River was London's main street. The streets were badly paved (sometimes unpaved) and so crowded that most people used the river if they wanted to get from one part of London to another. The noble houses along the Strand, the main road between London and Westminster, backed up to the river, and the residents kept their own boats at private docks. Ordinary citizens paid wherrymen (boatmen) to row them where they wanted to go. It was much quicker and cleaner than going by land.

Crowded Waterway

During Elizabeth's reign, however, the river was sometimes as difficult to navigate as the streets. This was especially true after 1558, when a law intended to control smuggling decreed that all foreign goods would be unloaded at approved docks, most of which were along a quarter mile of the bank near London Bridge. One contemporary observer wrote, "A man would say, that seeth the shipping there, that it is, as it were, a very wood [forest] of trees disbranched to make glades and let in light; so shaded is it with masts and sails."[40]

The river, however, was not much cleaner than the streets. Despite numerous attempts to stop the practice, people

dumped garbage and raw sewage into the Thames. Butchers used it to dispose of the bodies and unusable parts of cattle, sheep, and pigs. As a result, the Thames stank to the point where a visitor from Italy wrote that its "odour remains even in clean linen"[41] after being washed.

London Bridge was the only other way to cross the river. This marvelous structure was thought to be one of the wonders of the time. It was covered from bank to bank and lined with fashionable shops and houses. There was even a church halfway across. Above the gatehouse at the south end of London Bridge, the rotting heads of persons executed as traitors were stuck on poles. A visitor in 1594 counted thirty-four such grim reminders of the queen's justice.

In addition to serving as a house of worship, St. Paul's Cathedral served as the focal point for many social activities.

Yet for all its squalor, Elizabethan London could be an exciting place. The great theaters, including Shakespeare's Globe, were built in the suburbs on the south bank of the Thames. Even St. Paul's Cathedral, one of the largest churches in Europe, was lively. Besides being a house of worship, it was used as a place for business, gossip, plotting, and for lovers to meet. A visitor described the scene in Paul's Walk, the great middle aisle of the church:

> What swearing is there, what facing and out-facing? What shuffling, what shouldering, what jostling, what jeering, what biting of thumbs to beget quarrels . . . what casting open of cloaks to publish new clothes, what muffling in cloaks to hide broken elbows . . . foot by foot and elbow by elbow shall you see walking the knight, the gull, the gallant, the upstart, the gentleman, the clown, the captain, the apple-squire, the lawyer, the usurer, the citizen, the bankrupt, the scholar, the beggar, the doctor, the idiot, the ruffian, the cheater, the Puritan, the cut-throat.[42]

Goods for Sale

Everything was for sale in London. John Lyly described it in 1579 as "a place both for the beauty of building, infinite riches, variety of all things, that excelleth all the

Londoners

London was one of the largest and proudest cities in Europe during the Elizabethan era. This description was left by Duke Frederick of Würtenberg after a visit in 1592. It is found in Elizabethan People: State and Society, *edited by Joel Hurstfield and Alan G.R. Smith.*

[London] is a very populous city, so that one can scarcely pass along the streets, on account of the throng. The inhabitants are magnificently apparelled, and are extremely proud and overbearing; and because the greater part, especially the trades people, seldom go into other countries, but always remain in their houses in the city attending to their business, they care little for foreigners, but scoff and laugh at them; and moreover one dare not oppose them else the streetboys and apprentices collect together in immense crowds and strike to the right and left unmercifully without regard to person; and because they are the strongest, one is obliged to put up with the insult as well as the injury. The women have much more liberty than perhaps in any other place. They also know well how to make use of it, for they go dressed out in exceedingly fine clothes, and give all their attention to their ruffs and stuffs, to such a degree indeed, that, I am informed, many a one does not hesitate to wear velvet in the streets, which is common with them, whilst at home perhaps they have not a piece of dry bread.

cities in the world, insomuch that it may be called the storehouse and mart of all Europe."[43] London's version of the shopping mall was the Royal Exchange, built in 1567 as a place for merchants to show their wares. As a poem of the time said:

Such purses, gloves and points
Of cost and fashion rare,
Such cutworks, partlets, suits of lawn,
Bongraces and such ware;
Such gorgets, sleeves and ruffs,
Linings for gowns and cauls,
Coifs, cirppins, cornets, billaments,
Musk boxes and sweet balls;
Pincases, pick-tooths, beard-brushes,
Combs, needles, glasses, bells,
and many such like toys as these,
That Gain to Fancy sells.[44]

London was so much the center of business that other English cities complained. Merchants in Norwich, Bristol, Newcastle, Southampton, and the rest claimed London was swallowing the entire country's trade. One Bristol merchant grumbled that "God had no sons to whom he gave the benefits of the earth but in London."[45]

However, while it was true that merchants had to bring their goods to London to sell them to foreign buyers, they did, in fact, turn a tidy profit there that they took back home. Almost all the English cities prospered far more under Elizabeth than under her predecessors because of the growth of trade and manufacturing throughout the entire kingdom.

Urban Poverty

Not everyone in the cities prospered, however. While the wealth of the great merchants rivaled, and sometimes exceeded, that of the leading nobles, the bulk of the population had trouble making ends meet. During Elizabeth's reign, one of the problems first appearing in England was that of widespread urban poverty.

The cities were growing in independence. Elizabeth granted many more royal charters to cities and towns than did her predecessors. A charter set forth the extent to which a city could govern itself and be free from the authority of neighboring nobles. It also said what taxes, tolls, and other payments the cities could collect. The cities usually paid for these documents, providing the queen with revenue.

Part of the cities' growing power was their increased representation in Parliament. Elizabeth created thirty-two new boroughs, each of which had the right to send two members to Parliament. Because Parliament was not, under the Tudors, the all-powerful legislative body it would later become, the cities often let nearby landowners represent them—provided they could pay their own way. Only the largest cities were willing to pay the expenses for two members of Parliament, and few of the leading merchants were willing to leave their businesses and go to London to serve during a session that might last anywhere from a few weeks to half a year.

The cities, which for centuries had feuded mainly with local nobles, now argued instead with one another. Their new prosperity led to arguments over who had the right to fish in what waters, who had the right to sell what on market day, and who had the right to call out troops. The cities were jealous of the privileges they thought both tradition and their charters allowed them. Newcomers who wanted to set up businesses were not welcome. "Wherare other cities doe alure unto them goode workmen," wrote one haughty citizen, "our men will expell theim oute."[46]

While the cities dominated commerce, they did not, except for London, dominate the countryside around them. The most important accomplishment of the cities in the Elizabethan era was the measure of independence that was gained by the people. As historian A.L. Rowse writes, "The towns ran themselves, but they did not run the country."[47]

Chapter Four

The Question of Faith

When Elizabeth became queen, her subjects anxiously waited to see what form religion would take in England. Under her father and brother, the Church of England had replaced the Catholic Church as the state religion, but Catholicism was reinstated by Queen Mary I. The Church of England, as it emerged under Elizabeth, was an expression of her views and those of most of her people—moderate, conservative, and surprisingly tolerant. What came to be known as the Elizabethan Religious Settlement was to have a profound effect on the country.

Religion was the center of everyday life just as much in Elizabethan England as it had been for centuries. It raised passions like nothing else. People might be ardent Catholics, resolute Puritans, or even firm atheists (denying the existence of God), but almost no one was indifferent.

The English had been pulled this way and that over religion for twenty-five years. Not only were the people confused, they were also afraid. Hundreds of people, Catholic and Protestant, mighty and humble, had been executed for their beliefs. Above all, the people wanted and needed peace. The Duke of Norfolk advised Elizabeth, "Let your highness assure yourself that England can bear no more changes in religion. It hath been bowed so oft that if it should be bent again it would break."[48]

Elizabeth's Beliefs

Much depended on Elizabeth's personal beliefs. During her brother's reign, she had been a demure, pious Protestant. During her sister's, she attended Catholic mass dutifully, if unenthusiastically. Elizabeth's personal religion was a simple, rational belief that did not go to either Catholic or Protestant extremes. This middle-of-the-road approach was totally in keeping with the uncertainty through which Elizabeth had lived under both Edward and Mary. Once she wrote:

Christ was the word that spake it,
He took the bread and brake it;
And what his words did make it
That I believe and take it.[49]

Elizabeth was by no means tolerant of all Christians. She found both extreme Catholics and extreme Protestants distasteful. She took action against them, however, only when their beliefs posed a political threat, such as when some Catholics wanted to replace her with Mary, Queen of Scots, or when the Anabaptists, an extreme Protestant sect, preached complete separa-

Elizabeth kneels in prayer in this lithograph. Unlike her sister Mary, a religious zealot, Elizabeth adopted relatively moderate religious views.

The Oath of Supremacy

The first important step of Elizabeth's reign was to settle the question of whether England would be Catholic or Protestant. Under an act of Parliament in 1559, all churchmen and royal officials had to take the following oath, hand on the Bible, acknowledging her as head of the church. It is found in Elizabethan People: State and Society, *edited by Joel Hurstfield and Alan G.R. Smith.*

I, [name], do utterly testify and declare in my conscience that the Queen's Highness is the only supreme governor of this realm and of all other her Highness' dominions and countries, as well in all spiritual or ecclesiastical things or causes as temporal, and that no foreign prince, person, prelate, state or potentate hath or ought to have any jurisdiction, power, superiority, preeminence or authority ecclesiastical or spiritual within this realm, and therefore I do utterly renounce and forsake all foreign jurisdictions, powers, superiorities and authorities, and do promise that from henceforth I shall bear faith and free allegiance to the Queen's Highness, her heirs and lawful successors, and to my power shall assist and defend all jurisdictions, preeminences, privileges and authorities granted or belonging to the Queen's Highness, her heirs and successors, or united or annexed to the imperial crown of this realm: so help me God and by the contents of this Book.

tion of church and state. While between two and three hundred Catholics were executed during her reign, they had been charged with treason. Only four men—all Anabaptists—were burned at the stake for heresy, a crime against God.

Elizabeth probably could not have kept England Catholic even if she had wanted to. The persecutions under Queen Mary had produced a fierce hatred of Spain because the people believed she was guided by her Spanish husband and his Spanish advisers. Also, most of the leading merchants and gentry were firmly Protestant, and they were Elizabeth's strongest political supporters. In addition, one cannot see Elizabeth either embracing the religion that had called her a bastard (because it did not recognize Henry VIII's marriage to Anne Boleyn) or yielding any of her authority to foreign popes.

The Acts of Settlement

The country soon had its answer. The Acts of Settlement were enacted by Parliament in 1559. They consisted of two primary measures—the Act of Supremacy and the Act of Uniformity. The Act of Supremacy required all church and government officials to swear absolute loyalty to Elizabeth as supreme governor of the church. A similar law had been passed by Henry VIII, but Henry's title had been supreme head of the church. Elizabeth had no wish to make herself the final authority on matters of faith, once proclaiming that she "refused to make windows into men's souls."[50] She was far more interested in political rather than spiritual control. Nearly all the bishops, all of whom had been created by Mary, remained loyal to the pope, refused to take the oath, and were deprived of their offices. Ordinary priests, however, accepted the settlement. Only about two hundred of an estimated six thousand refused.

The Act of Uniformity was intended to make church services the same throughout the country. Elizabeth wanted to control the service so that it would not be too Catholic or too Protestant in character and thus would appeal to most of the people. The prayer book written during Edward VI's reign was reissued. It was not as extremely Protestant as the original and added language designed to appeal to Catholics. It succeeded in appealing to a wide range of Elizabeth's subjects. Only the most radical Protestants (the Puritans) and the most uncompromising Catholics (called *recusants*) objected.

The Act of Uniformity also regulated what priests would wear and many other outward forms of religion. It also permitted priests to marry, unlike the Catholic Church, and made church attendance compulsory. Every person was supposed to attend church in his or her home parish. Those who did not attend were fined.

The Acts of Settlement were followed in 1563 by the Thirty-nine Articles, the formal statement of beliefs of the Church of England. They put Elizabeth's church squarely in the middle of Christianity's theological road. They reduced the traditional seven Catholic sacraments to two—baptism and holy communion. They rejected the Catholic doctrine of purgatory, which held that those who had received God's grace, but had died in sin, required a time of purification before entering heaven.

Grace Through Faith

God's grace itself, however, as bestowed on the basis of faith alone, and not of good conduct or charity, was acknowledged as the only path to heaven, following the doctrine of Martin Luther, the German monk who had begun the Protestant Reformation. Also rejected were the Catholic doctrines that God's grace can be earned by confession or penance or conferred by the church.

Historian S.T. Bindoff writes that the Elizabethan church "was designed to appeal to a lukewarm multitude and it enlisted their lukewarm support. . . . [While] it lit no fires to consume men's bodies . . . it also kindled no flame in men's hearts."[51] Flaming religious zeal, however, was the last thing England needed, and Elizabeth knew it.

The Elizabethan Religious Settlement concentrated on external worship instead of internal faith, whereas in other parts of Europe—especially in Spain—people suspected of having departed in the least from the established belief were tortured and burned at the stake. As long as England's people conformed outwardly, they could believe much as they wanted to.

The concept that differences in religious beliefs were acceptable was revolutionary. Throughout European history, any departure from the established system of belief laid down by the Catholic Church had been heresy. Elizabeth, in saying that "there is only one Jesus Christ and all the rest is a

A mother and her daughter pose for a christening portrait. The Church of England retained only two of the traditional seven Catholic sacraments: baptism and holy communion.

dispute over trifles,"[52] came close to saying that a different form of worship was not necessarily evil. Complete freedom of religion still was a long way off, but the first step—an acknowledgment that people might still be good Christians although their beliefs differed slightly from those of their neighbors—had been taken.

The Iconoclasts

Elizabeth's "trifles," the outward expressions of religion, still meant a great deal to some people. In their eagerness to erase Catholicism, the more extreme Protestants destroyed countless works of art considered symbols of "popery"—paintings, crucifixes, statues, tombs. A Puritan in Kent was delighted "to deface a monument of superstition, to put away a font-cast, coloured, gilded and pictures story-like with the seven popish sacraments . . . a great offence to all that are Christianly minded."[53]

The great majority of the people, however, did not want to see the outward forms of Catholicism erased. Religion, to them, was not a matter of great theological debates but rather what they experienced in church every Sunday. Most had been raised as Catholics and found comfort in the ancient symbols and ceremonies.

Elizabeth was wise enough to realize this, and her Church of England retained many of what the more radical Protestants called "rags of popery." Bishops still maintained great houses. Priests still wore vestments. The traditional saints were still venerated, and most of their statues survived, as did the jeweled crosses. The entire Anglican service, in fact, was patterned closely after the traditional Catholic mass.

The English may have lost relics and monuments through the Elizabethan settlement, but they gained something more valuable in the long run—the Bible. The Bible had been translated into English under Henry VIII, who put copies in every church and then refused to permit ordinary people to read them. The word of God, he thought, was not to be debated, except by scholars. The English Bible had

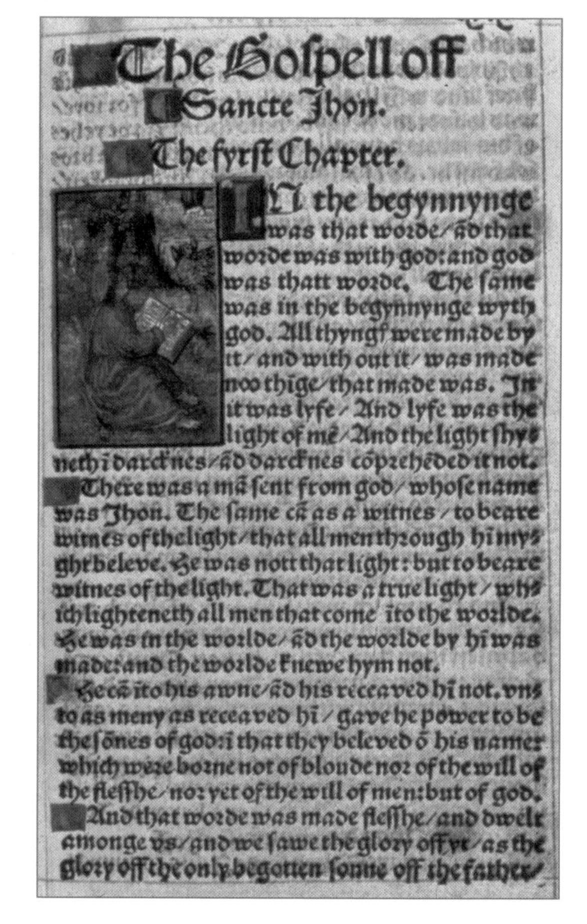
The Gospell off
Sancte Jhon.
The fyrſt Chapter.
IN the begynnynge was that worde/ãd that worde was with god: and god was thatt worde. The ſame was in the begynnynge wyth god. All thyngſ were made by it/ and with out it/ was made noo thĩge/ that made was. In it was lyfe/ And lyfe was the light of mẽ/ And the light ſhyneth ĩ darcknes/ ãd darcknes cõprehẽded it not.
There was a mã ſent from god/ whoſe name was Jhon. The ſame cã as a witnes/ to beare witnes of the light/ that all men through hĩ myght beleve. He was nott that light: but to beare witnes of the light. That was a true light/ which lighteneth all men that come ĩto the worlde. He was in the worlde/ ãd the worlde by hĩ was made: and the worlde knewe hym not.
He cã ĩto his awne/ ãd his receaved hĩ not. vnto as meny as receaved hĩ/ gave he power to be the ſõnes of god: ĩ that they beleved õ his name: which were borne not of bloude nor of the will of the fleſſhe/ nor yet of the will of men: but of god.
And that worde was made fleſſhe/ and dwelt amonge vs/ and we ſawe the glory off yt/ as the glory off the only begotten ſonne off the father/

This page is taken from a sixteenth-century English translation of the Gospel of Saint John.

been banned by Mary, but Elizabeth, after great hesitation, permitted it, not only in churches but also in homes.

Throughout Elizabeth's reign, thousands learned to read so they could read the Bible for themselves. Bible reading became a family pastime. As more people read the Bible, they discussed what it meant. Priests were asked to explain certain passages. The sermon became a feature of the Church of England service. Some congregations thought the service incomplete unless the sermon lasted three hours.

The Power of the Clergy

Regardless of what they wore or what they preached, churchmen were far less powerful under Elizabeth that during any previous reign, even that of her father. She depended on the bishops to keep firm control of religious matters, and she kept a firm control on them. The nineteenth-century historian James Anthony Froude wrote that when a bishop grew too independent, the queen would send a courtier to remind him that "she is right [truly] King Henry, her father, if any strive with her."[54] If the bishop persisted, he might suddenly find himself the object of an official investigation into his expenditures.

Elizabeth refused to let clergymen dictate to her, either in great matters or small ones. She personally disliked sermons, thinking they bred too much independent thought, and once said she considered three or four preachers enough for her entire kingdom. Consequently, it was a brave or foolhardy priest who was critical of anything remotely touching the queen or the court. The Bishop of London once was foolish enough to preach on "the vanitie of decking the body too finely"[55] when the queen was present. She promptly walked out of the service, saying that, "if the bishope helde more discourse on such matters she woold fitte him for heaven."[56]

The Elizabethan Religious Settlement was one of the most important aspects of Elizabeth's reign. First, as Rowse writes, it provided "the maximum amount of unity for the English people that could be

A Typical Parish

By far, most of the people of England during the Elizabethan era had neither the narrowness of the Puritans nor the religious fervor of the Catholics. Instead, their worship was conventional and matter of fact, as this passage by Nicholas Breton shows. It is found in Elizabethan People: State and Society, *edited by Joel Hurstfield and Alan G.R. Smith.*

And for my parishioners, they are a kind of people that love a pot of ale better than a pulpit, and a corn-rick better than a church-door, who, coming to divine service more for fashion than devotion, are contented after a little capping and kneeling, coughing and spitting, to help me to sing out a psalm, and sleep at the second lesson, or awake to stand up at the gospel, and say 'Amen' at the peace of God, and stay till the banns of matrimony be asked, or till the clerk have cried a pied stray bullock, a black sheep or a gray mare, and then, for that some dwell far off, be glad to be gotten home to dinner.

Pope Pius V excommunicated Elizabeth and urged Catholics to rebel against her to force England to return to Catholicism.

combined with probably the greatest amount of liberty of opinion that was possible under the circumstances."[57] Second, it served as a great intellectual stimulation. Permitted a range of beliefs and the reading of the Bible, more people began to think for themselves. Third, it provided a system of belief and a moral guide—one that set forth a general code of conduct that depended on individual conscience rather than on hard and fast rules—that was in keeping with the independent, broad-minded character of the English.

The Catholics

The Catholics, at first, could exist under this system. Later in the reign, however, threats from abroad ended what a contemporary historian called the "calm and quiet season."[58] These threats, which included plots to kill Elizabeth and put Mary, Queen of Scots, on the throne, brought an increase in anti-Catholic laws. Then, in 1570, Pope Pius V, hoping to force a rebellion through which England would become Catholic once more, issued a decree excommunicating Elizabeth, declaring her deposed from the English throne, and calling on all faithful Catholics to rebel against her.

People's private beliefs were one thing to Elizabeth, but this was a direct challenge to her rule. Reaction was swift. The Catholic mass was forbidden, even in secret. Royal commissioners toured the country again, renewing the Oath of Supremacy. In addition, suspected Catholics were asked whether, if England were invaded by a Catholic country, they would fight for the queen. Catholics, if they answered this "Bloody Question" with no, were traitors. Cuthbert Mayne, a priest who answered that all Catholics should fight, instead, for the invaders, was hanged.

Catholic Europe increased the pressure on England in 1580 by sending into the country young English Catholics who had gone into exile and become Jesuits, members of the Society of Jesus. The mission of the Jesuits, whom Elizabeth's government outlawed, was to move secretly throughout the country—preaching, distributing Catholic literature, and urging rebellion. One of the Jesuit leaders, Edmund Campion, proclaimed his goal was "of free cost to preach the Gospel, to minister the Sacraments, to instruct the simple, to reform sinners, to confute errors—in brief, to cry alarm spiritual against foul vice and proud ignorance, wherewith many my dear countrymen are abused."[59]

The government went all out to stop the Jesuits. Heavy fines were imposed for both saying and attending a Catholic mass. Wealthy Catholics saw their lands confiscated. Jesuits were hunted down and executed for treason. Still, fewer people were executed solely for their religion in thirty years of Elizabeth's reign than in the last three years of her sister's.

The vast majority of Catholics remained loyal to Elizabeth. The attempted invasion by Spain in 1588 depended on England's Catholics rising up against their queen. This would have been most unlikely. They were Englishmen first, Catholics second.

The Puritans

No less extreme a religious sect were the Puritans. Though they did not pose the same threat as the Catholics, Elizabeth liked them even less. The Puritan movement began when some Protestant exiles during Mary's reign settled in Geneva, Switzerland, and came under the influence of John Calvin. They believed that all aspects of life should center around the church and that all public and private actions should be directed toward God. Each person, the Puritans believed, could grow nearer to God by living as sober and pious a life as possible.

Consequently, Puritans lived strict, grim lives. Not only did they disapprove of images in churches, but they also wished to eliminate most holidays, including Christmas. Dancing, card playing, and sports of any kind were thought to be evil. The Puritans' recreation was praying, fasting, reading religious texts, and listening to sermons. They not only lived this way, but they also wanted everyone else to. No wonder Elizabeth hated them!

It was not only the Puritans' severe lifestyle, however, that aroused Elizabeth's ire. They rejected the Anglican hierarchy of bishops, preferring, instead, the Presbyterian system that existed in Scotland that made each congregation virtually independent. To the Puritan, religion was everything, and a person's individual conscience took precedence over any earthly power—even that of the queen.

Elizabeth could not abide such a notion, striking as it did at the very roots of her authority. In her view, the church was part of the state, and a subordinate part at that. The Puritans, on the other hand, held that

A Puritan Lady's Day

Religion was a vital part of every day's activities to the Puritans, as shown by this excerpt from the Diary of Lady Margaret Hoby, *a Yorkshire woman. It is found in* Elizabethan People: State and Society, *edited by Joel Hurstfield and Alan G.R. Smith.*

In the morning after private prayers and order taken for dinner I wrote some notes in my Testament till 10 o'clock; then I went to walk and, after I returned home, I prayed privately, read a chapter of the Bible, and wrought [embroidered] till dinner time. After, I walked awhile with Mr Rhodes [her chaplain] and this I wrought and did some good things about the house till 4. Then I wrote out the sermon into my book preached the day before and, when I had again gone about in the house and given order for supper and other things, I returned to examination and prayer. Then I walked till supper time and, after catechising [studying scripture], meditated awhile of that I had heard, with mourning to God for pardon both of my omission and commission wherein I found myself guilty, I went to bed.

In keeping with their austere vision of life, most Puritans, like this woman, dressed in plain, dark clothing.

everything—the government included—existed only to serve God.

Whitgift's Task

John Whitgift, archbishop of Canterbury in the 1580s, was ordered by the queen to limit the efforts of the Puritans to reform the Church of England according to their own views. He did so by forcing Puritan clergymen to accept the Church of England prayer book as containing nothing "contrary in some points to the Holy Scriptures."[60] If they refused, they were removed and fined. He also punished Puritan writers and closed down the printers who published their works.

Whitgift was successful. The Puritan movement was suppressed for the time being. However, it was so popular among the middle class, including the leading merchants, that it would grow even stronger after Elizabeth's death. The conflict would become so great that official persecution would drive many Puritans to leave England, including those who established themselves in North America.

Eventually, about fifty years after Elizabeth's death, the Puritans gained complete political control of England, but they did not hold it long. One of the great accomplishments of Elizabeth was that, by acting to limit the power of both the Catholics and the Puritans, she gave the Church of England—created under her father and given substance under her brother—time to grow strong enough to survive.

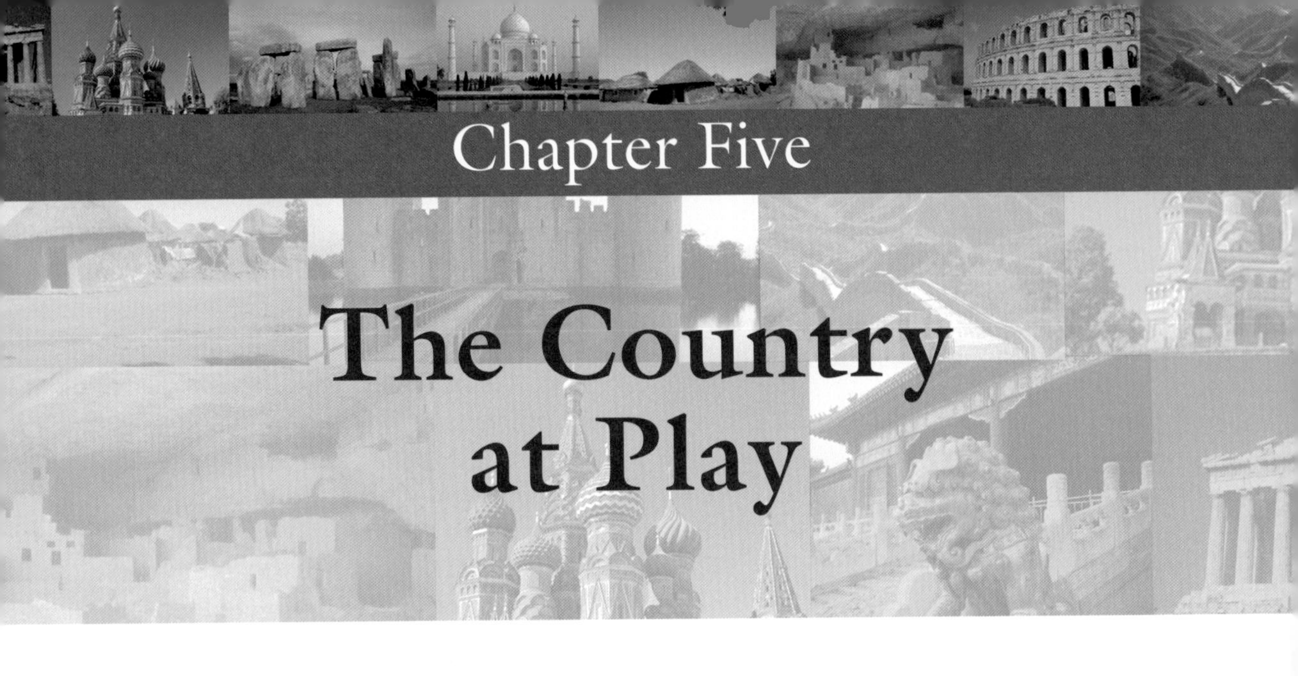

Chapter Five

The Country at Play

The people of the Elizabethan era had a zest for living. They worked hard, and they played just as hard. Their lives were crude, rough, and often violent, and so were their pastimes.

In earlier centuries, sports served primarily as training for battle. In contrast, the Elizabethan gentleman viewed sports as pleasant, but important, pastimes, and people of all classes found participation in sports a source of amusement. Roger Ascham, Elizabeth's tutor while she was a young lady, urged young men

> to ride comely, to run fair at the tilt or ring [trying to hit a target with a lance while on horseback], to play at all weapons, to shoot fair in bow, or surely in gun; to vault lustily, to run, to leap, to wrestle, to swim; to dance comely, to sing, and play of instruments cunningly; to hawk, to hunt, to play at tennis, and all pastimes generally which be joined with labour, used in open place, and on the day light, containing either some fit exercise for war, or some pleasant pastime for peace.[61]

Hunting was the most popular sport for all classes. England was still very rural and mostly open. Deer hunting was the favorite sport of the upper classes, as it had been for centuries. Common people were forbidden by law to hunt deer, and the poor man who killed one to feed his family could be hanged. Great nobles hunted on their own lands and sometimes kept deer parks, sections of forest set aside specifically for raising and hunting deer. In the chase, deer were flushed from hiding with packs of dogs and then pursued on horseback. When, at last, the deer fell exhausted, the first hunter to reach it would kill it by slitting its throat.

The Drive

Another method of deer hunting was the drive. Servants, beating the bushes with sticks and making loud noises, drove the deer toward the edge of a wood or a clearing where hunters waited with bows and arrows. This was a sport for the less adventuresome and for those like poet George Gascoigne, who might have considered racing around the countryside on horseback a bit vulgar: "A sport for noble peers, a sport for gentle bloods, The pain I leave for servants such as beat the bushy woods." [62]

Elizabeth enjoyed this form of hunting as she grew older, but she still loved the thrill of the chase. At age sixty-seven, she still could occasionally be found hunting on horseback.

Ordinary people enjoyed hunting, too. They were free to hunt the foxes, badgers, squirrels, otters, and hares that could be found throughout the countryside. "Coursing" the hares was extremely popular. Hares were captured and then given

Led by huntsmen and dogs, a noblewoman and her ladies-in-waiting embark on a hunting expedition.

A sixteenth-century engraving shows Queen Elizabeth I on the hunt. The queen loved hunting and participated in the sport well into her late sixties.

a twelve-yard head start over a pack of greyhounds. The object was to see who had the fastest dogs.

Game birds, such as quail, pheasant, and grouse, were plentiful, and the favorite way of hunting them was with falcons or hawks. Like deer hunting, falconry and hawking were sports for the wealthy. Birds were very expensive. Sir Walter Raleigh once wrote to Robert Cecil, Lord Burghley's son, "If you will be so bountiful to give another falcon, I will provide you a running gelding [a horse]."[63] Falcons hunted by soaring far above their masters, then diving in for the kill when dogs flushed game birds from hiding.

Fishing

Fishing appealed to those who enjoyed a less active, more peaceful pastime. Many rivers were full of salmon. Some towns farmed nearby streams, stretching nets across them to trap the fish. Individuals preferred "angling," fishing with hook and line. Anglers either used "still fishing," dropping baited hooks into the water, or "fly fishing," tying feathers onto hooks to make them look like insects and then casting them over the water. Then, as now, fishing was a way to get away from it all. Elizabethan Richard Carew wrote:

> I wait not at the lawyers' gates,
> Nor shoulder climbers down the stairs;
> I vault not manhood by debates,
> I envy not the miser's fears:
> But mean in state and calm in sprite,
> My full fish-pond is my delight.[64]

Horse racing became popular in England under Henry VIII and continued under Elizabeth. Books on horse breeding and training were published during her reign, and for the first time the landed gentry as well as the nobility raced horses. Many towns built tracks and organized series of races to which owners brought their horses. Although owning and racing horses was only for the wealthy, people of the towns flocked to see and bet on the races, making it one of England's few spectator sports.

Blood Sports

Other spectator sports included violent blood sports such as bearbaiting, bullbaiting, and cockfighting. The animals to be baited—bears, bulls, and sometimes even lions or apes—would be held by a length of chain to a stake, and dogs—bulldogs or mastiffs—would be set loose on them. The dogs would rush in and try to seize the larger animals in their strong jaws before they could be clawed, gored, or swatted away. The dogs won if the larger animal was killed. They lost if so many of them were disabled that the rest refused to attack.

Cockfighting was another popular sport. Roosters were fitted with sharp blades on each foot and put into a pit to fight to the death. Fighting cocks, like falcons, were expensive. It took a well-to-do man (cockfighting seems to have been an all-male pastime) to own cocks, but men of all classes came to see and bet on the fights.

The blood sports, thought by most people today to be too gruesome, cruel, and violent, had great appeal for the Elizabethans.

Elizabethans particularly loved bloody spectator sports such as bearbaiting and bullbaiting, in which they bet on the outcome.

Large crowds of both men and women of all classes flocked to see baiting, and Elizabeth frequently used it to entertain visiting ambassadors. "The average Elizabethan," writes historian Muriel St. Clair Byrne, "was not sensitive to the spectacle of physical suffering, either in human beings or in animals."[65]

Team Sports

Team sports gained in popularity during Elizabeth's reign, and they were just as rough and violent as those involving animals. The two most played by common men (but not women) were hurling and football.

Both were ball games. Hurling was like a combination of hockey and polo. Some players were on foot; others, on horseback. The object of the game was to strike a ball so that it went over the opponents' goal. The ball was struck toward the goal by a stick or club. Hurling was more organized in towns, with up to thirty men on a side and definite goals to cross. Country hurling might match the entire adult male populations of two villages, and the goals might be 3 or 4 miles (4.8 or 6.4km) apart.

Football (not an ancestor of American football, despite the similarities) got its name not because the ball was kicked but because all the players went on foot. The ball was carried, and whoever carried it became a target for tacklers. As in hurling, the "field" often was the countryside between two villages. Football was incredibly violent, with few or no rules. John Stubbes wrote:

> Doth not everyone lie in wait for his adversary, seeking to overthrow him and to pitch him on the nose, though it be upon hard stones, in ditch or dale, in valley or hill, or what place soever it be, he careth not, so he have him down? And he that can serve the most of this fashion, he is counted the only fellow . . . so that by this means sometimes their necks are broken, sometimes their backs, sometimes their legs, sometimes their arms; sometime one part thrust out of joint, sometime another; sometime the noses gush out with blood, sometime their eyes start out.[66]

Sports for a Gentleman

In Lord Herbert of Cherbury's (1583–1648) autobiography, he gives his opinion on what sort of pastimes are fit for gentlemen and which are not. This passage is from Elizabethan People: State and Society, *edited by Joel Hurstfield and Alan G.R. Smith.*

It will be fit for a gentleman also to learn to swim, unless he be given to cramps and convulsions; howbeit, I must confess, in my own particular, that I cannot swim; for, as I was once in danger of drowning, by learning to swim, my mother, upon her blessing, charged me never to learn swimming. . . . It will be good also for a gentleman to learn to leap, wrestle, and vault on horseback; they being all of them qualities of great use. I do much approve likewise of shooting in the long-bow, as being both an healthful exercise and useful for the wars, notwithstanding all that our firemen [gunners] speak against it; for, bring an hundred archers against so many musqueteers, I say if the archer comes within his distance, he will not only make two shoots, but two hits for one. The exercises I do not approve of are riding of running horses, there being much cheating in that kind; neither do I see why a brave man should delight in a creature whose chief use is to help him to run away. . . . The exercises I wholly condemn, are dicing and carding, especially if you play for any great sum of money, or spend any time in them; or use to come to meetings in dicing-houses where cheaters meet and cozen [cheat] young gentlemen of all of their money.

Sports on Sundays

The main reason that Stubbes, a Puritan, disliked football was that it was played on Sunday, when the Puritans thought everyone should be either in church or in spiritual meditation. He wrote, "Any exercise which withdraweth us from godliness, either upon the sabbath or any other day, is wicked and to be forbidden."[67]

The government objected to it also, but only because it took time away from archery. The government felt men were spending too much time playing football and too little practicing with bow and arrow. The longbow had been England's chief weapon of war for two hundred years, and both Henry VIII and Elizabeth made archery practice mandatory for all able-bodied villagers.

This woodcut shows the Globe Theater in Southwark, where many of Shakespeare's plays debuted.

Fencing, enjoyed by the nobles, was another sport left over from warfare. The English had always preferred the broadsword and buckler (a small, round shield), but the long, slim rapier became fashionable during the Elizabethan era, largely because it was more elegant to wear. Playwright Henry Porter lamented, "Sword and buckler fight begin to grow out of use. I am sorry for it. I shall never see good manhood again. If it be once gone, this poking fight with rapier and dagger will come up. Then the tall man will be spitted like a cat or a rabbit."[68]

On the more refined side, dancing was popular with everyone except, of course, the Puritans, who believed it was sinful. Elizabeth was passionately fond of dancing. She once asked a French ambassador who was the better dancer, herself or Mary, Queen of Scots? The ambassador of course replied that Mary "danced not so high and disposedly as she did."[69]

The Theater

The cultural pastime for which the Elizabethan era is best known, however, is the theater. Commoners and nobles loved plays, no one more than the queen. Her enthusiasm for plays led to the flowering of English drama. Roving bands of actors had been popular in England for many years, but the plays themselves had been little more than melodramas or slapstick comedies. The more sophisticated audiences of Elizabeth's court wanted plays of higher quality. This demand, in turn, motivated the writing of some of the greatest works in the English language, most notably by Christopher Marlowe and William Shakespeare.

A Royal Performance?

According to one story of doubtful authenticity, Queen Elizabeth once not only attended a performance of a Shakespeare play at one of the famous theaters south of London but also even went on stage.

The best seats in the house were literally on the stage and off to one side. They were especially popular with male courtiers who liked to show off the fine clothes they were wearing.

The story goes that the queen, while occupying one of these seats, grew so bored with the performance that she got up and strolled leisurely through the actors to the other side. When the actors ignored her and carried on with the play, she walked back across and dropped a glove at Shakespeare's feet.

The playwright supposedly picked it up, offered it to the queen with a flourish, and said, "And though now bent on this high embassy/Yet stoop we to take up our Cousin's glove," whereupon the audience burst out in applause.

The story, which is found in *All the Queen's Men* by Peter Brimacombe, is very improbable. Elizabeth would have been extremely unlikely to have gone to a public theater. When she saw plays, they were usually brought to the palace or performed in the houses of great nobles.

The queen's sponsorship not only fueled creativity among playwrights but also perhaps saved drama from being snuffed out. The Puritans, increasingly numerous and powerful in England, despised the theater as ungodly, but they could not eliminate it

The Wicked Theater

The upright merchants of London frowned on the theater since it tended to distract people from work and worship. This passage is from an act of London's city council in 1574. It is found in The Horizon Book of the Elizabethan World *by Lacey Baldwin Smith, edited by Norman Kotler.*

Sundry great disorders and inconveniences have been found to ensue to this city by the inordinate haunting of great multitudes of people, especially youth, to plays, interludes, and shows—namely, occasion of frays and quarrels; evil practices of incontinency in great inns have chambers and secret places adjoining to their open stages and galleries; inveigling and alluring of maids, specially orphans and good citizens' children under age, to privy and unmeet contracts; the publishing of unchaste, uncomely, and unshamefast speeches and doings; withdrawing of the queen's majesty's subjects from divine service on Sundays and holidays, at which times such plays were chiefly used; unthrifty waste of the money of the poor and found persons; sundry robberies by picking and cutting of purses; uttering of popular, busy, and seditious matters; and many other corruptions of youth and other enormities—besides that also sundry slaughters and mayhemings of the queen's subjects have happened by ruins of scaffolds, frames, and stages, and by engines, weapons, and powder used in plays."

so long as their monarch viewed it, as she put it, "as well for the recreation of our loving subjects as for our solace and pleasure."[70]

It was during Elizabeth's reign that the first permanent theaters were built on the south bank of the Thames in Southwark. Among them was the famous Globe, where many of Shakespeare's works were first performed. The queen, however, would not have attended a performance there—virtually no lady of quality did. Instead, the theater companies would have come to the palace, as they did when *Twelfth Night* made its debut at Hampton Court.

Although they could be complex and subtle, there was little about Elizabethan plays that could be called dainty or refined. The comedies, which the queen loved best, were bawdy. She was attracted to the character of Falstaff in Shakespeare's *King Henry V, Part II,* and wondered aloud what it would be like if Falstaff fell in love. The result was the rollicking *Merry Wives of Windsor.*

Likewise, audiences expected the tragedies and histories to be full of action and as lifelike as possible. Violent death was an integral part of these plays, and to make it seem real, the master of the revels, who arranged the performances and was responsible for helping find necessary props, including legs and arms so lifelike as to, when "cut off" in a stage battle, spurt what appeared to be blood.

Poetry

In addition to drama, poetry flourished in Elizabeth's court, much of it directed at her. One of the hallmarks of the accomplished courtier was the ability to write verse, and some of the most outstanding poets of the age, such as Sir Walter Raleigh and Sir Philip Sidney, were talented amateurs whose official duties at court lay elsewhere. On the other hand, writers such as Edmund Spenser were professionals, who had to depend on the support of the queen and other nobles to earn their keep.

Not all members of the court, however, were strong patrons of the arts. For example, the thrifty William Cecil, when told by the queen to pay Spenser one hundred pounds for a collection of poems, groused, "What! All this for a song?"[71]

Entertainment of an even less-refined sort was provided by court jesters, or fools, as they were commonly known. Elizabeth had several during her reign, but her favorite and easily the most famous was Dick Tarleton, who was adept at reading the queen's moods and knew just what to say to lift her spirits. Her courtiers knew this and sometimes employed him to soften Elizabeth before they sought some favor. Thomas Fuller, writing during the next century, related that when the queen

> was serious (I dare not say sullen) and out of good humour, he [Tarleton] could un-dumpish her at his pleasure. Her highest Favourites, would in some Cases, go to Tarleton, before they would go to the Queen, and he was their Usher to prepare their advantageous access unto Her. In a word, He told the Queen more of her faults, than most of her Chaplains, and cured her Melancholy better than all of her physicians.[72]

Jugglers, acrobats, and other such entertainers also performed for the court. Robert Laneham, in his account of Elizabeth's

Sir Philip Sidney was a courtier and devoted amateur poet, one of many in Elizabeth's court.

progress to Dudley's estate at Kenilworth, described an Italian contortionist who put on a show "with sundry windings, gyrings and circumflexions; all so lightly and with such ease as by me, in a few words, it is not expressible by pen or speech. . . . [I] began to doubt whether it was a man or a spirit metalled [with a back] like a lamprey, that has no bone, but a line like a lute string."[73]

Games and Gambling

Sometimes the members of the court would amuse themselves with card, board, or dice games, often gambling much more than they could afford to lose. Playing cards with Elizabeth could be especially expensive since she did not like to lose and her opponents usually saw to it that she did not. Her favorite card game was one called

Gentlemen play a hand of primero, a popular gambling card game in Elizabeth's court and a favorite of the queen's.

Inhabitants of a village near London take part in a celebration. People of all classes loved holiday feasts and entertainment.

primero, and one of her frequent opponents was Lord North. His household accounts show regular entries of sums as large as seventy pounds, about ten thousand dollars, "lost to the queen at play."[74]

The calendar was full of festivals and feasts for all classes. Almost all were church holidays, although some originated in pre-Christian customs. The use of mistletoe and a Yule log went back thousands of years. In some areas, people danced at dawn on Easter Sunday, not realizing the practice dated back to sun worshipping. In one country parish, a bull was sacrificed to a patron saint.

Rural English churches were places for fun as well as for faith. When churches needed new roofs or windows, the money was usually raised through church ales. Nearby farmers donated malt, and a very strong ale was brewed and sold to people who came from miles around to buy it. The more one drank, the greater the gift to God. One writer said, "Then when . . . this duff cap [ale] . . . is set abroach, well is he that can get the soonest to it and spend the most at it; for he that sitteth the closest to it and spends the most at it, he is counted the godliest man of all the rest."[75]

Elizabethan Christmas

Christmas was the greatest of all festivals. Feasting and dancing lasted twelve days—from Christmas Eve to Twelfth Night. Masques, plays, and feasts were held each night at court and in the houses of the nobles and the gentry. Even in the houses of the common people, it was a time for merrymaking and as rich food as was affordable, including the traditional Christmas dishes of roast goose, plum pudding, and wassail, a spiced wine. Everyone exchanged gifts on New Year's Day. One year, as described by John Nichols in an account of the queen's progresses, Leicester gave Elizabeth a "very fair jewel of gold, being a clock fully furnished with small diamonds and an apple of gold enameled green and russet."[76] Even the poorest people exchanged gifts, often no more than an apple or an orange.

The sports and pastimes of Elizabethan England were challenged in the next century by the Puritans. When the Puritan Parliament ruled England during the Commonwealth (1647–1660), Christmas and most other holidays were abolished. Games and plays were forbidden. But the spirit of the Elizabethan era proved to be too strong, and the country gladly welcomed back both its king and its customs.

Chapter Six

Science, Medicine, and Superstition

Distinguished Elizabethan historian A.L. Rowse calls the Renaissance "a betwixt and between world."[77] This was especially true of science during the Elizabethan era. Although a handful of brilliant men made momentous strides, such as William Harvey's discovery of the circulation of blood, most people still believed in magic and witchcraft. Historian Lacey Baldwin Smith writes:

> Sixteenth-century scientific truth was a strange composite of the old and new, chemistry and alchemy, astronomy and astrology, mathematics and numerology, medicine and magic, observation and sorcery. A bold mind might lift a corner of the curtain of ignorance and glimpse the truth, but the man who dismissed astrology as nonsense might himself be a helpless devotee of occultism and cabala.[78]

Dr. John Dee was a perfect example. The son of a Welsh tailor who made clothes for Henry VIII and members of his court, Dee began studying the movements of the stars while a student at Cambridge University. He was equally versed in mathematics, and in 1546 he became a founding fellow of Trinity College, Cambridge.

Dee left England to travel and study elsewhere in Europe, returning in 1551, but such was the state of science in England that he was arrested in 1555 for "calculating," mathematics being thought by some to be close to sorcery. He was the outstanding scientist of the first part of Elizabeth's reign, inventing new types of compasses and editing the English translation of the works of the Greek mathematician Euclid. In the introduction to his translation, he writes:

> O comfortable allurement, O ravishing persuasion to deal with a science whose subject is so ancient, so pure, so excellent, so surrounding all creatures, so used of the almighty and incomprehensible wisdom of the Creator, in distinct creation of all

The most famous scientist of the early years of Elizabeth's reign, John Dee was appointed the queen's personal astrologer.

> creatures: in all their distinct parts, properties, natures, and virtues, by order, and most absolute number, brought from nothing to the formality of their being and state.[79]

Astrology

Dee was devoted, however, to astrology—the prediction of events from the position of the stars, sun, moon, and planets—and was Queen Elizabeth's personal astrologer. In his later years, he became involved in crystal-ball gazing and in alchemy—attempting to turn metals like lead or mercury into gold. Eventually, people considered him more of a wizard than a scientist, and in 1583, while he was away, a mob attacked his house, burned his library, and stole all his equipment.

Astrology, however, was so much a way of life that it became part of the language. We still speak of someone "born under a lucky star." Elizabeth once wrote to Mary, Queen of Scots, "I consider that by nature we are composed of earthly elements and governed by heavenly, and . . . I am not ignorant that our dispositions are caused in part by supernatural signs."[80]

Elizabethans used astrology both to predict the future and to try to control it. The queen had Dee cast the horoscopes—predictions based on the stars—of some of her various suitors. She asked him to consult his charts of the stars and planets before deciding on a day for her coronation, wanting to choose a day that would ensure a prosperous reign. When Elizabeth lay near death with smallpox in 1562, courtiers—wanting to be on the winning side—rushed to astrologers, asking them to cast the horoscopes of possible heirs to the throne. Astrologers were consulted even in small matters. Dee's clients sought his help in finding lost items—everything from a gold ring to a sack of flour.

Astrology was considered vital to agriculture. Farmers planted crops according to the heavens. Thomas Tusser, whose

Defending Copernicus

Mathematician Thomas Digges, in his 1576 paper entitled Prognostication Everlasting, *corrected the work of his father, Leonard, and defended the position of astronomer Nicolaus Copernicus, who had proposed that the earth and planets revolve around the sun. This passage is from* Elizabethan People: State and Society, *edited by Joel Hurstfield and Alan G.R. Smith.*

Having of late . . . corrected and reformed sundry faults that by negligence in printing have crept into my father's *General Prognostication*, among other things I found a description or model of the world and situation of spheres celestial and elementary according to the doctrine of Ptolomey [an ancient Egyptian astronomer], whereunto all universities (led thereto chiefly by the authority of Aristotle [an ancient Greek philosopher]) since then have consented. But in our age one rare wit (seeing the continual errors that from time to time more and more have been discovered, besides the infinite absurdities in their theorickes, which they have been forced to admit that would not confess any mobility in the ball of the earth) hath by long study, painful practice, and rare invention delivered a new theorick or model of the world, shewing that the earth resteth not in the centre of the whole world, but only in the centre of this our mortal world or globe of elements, which environed and enclosed in the moon's orb, and together with the whole globe of mortality is carried yearly round the sun, which like a king in the midst of all reigneth and giveth the laws of motion to the rest, spherically dispersing his glorious beams of light through all this sacred celestial temple. . . . So many ways is the sense of mortal men abused, but reason and deep discourse of wit having opened these things to Copernicus.

agricultural poetry and proverbs include the famous rhyme "Sweet April showers do bring May flowers," told them:

> Sow [peas] and beans in the
> wane of the moon,
> Who soweth them sooner, he
> soweth too soon;
> That they with the planet may
> rest and arise
> And flourish with bearing most
> plentiful wise.[81]

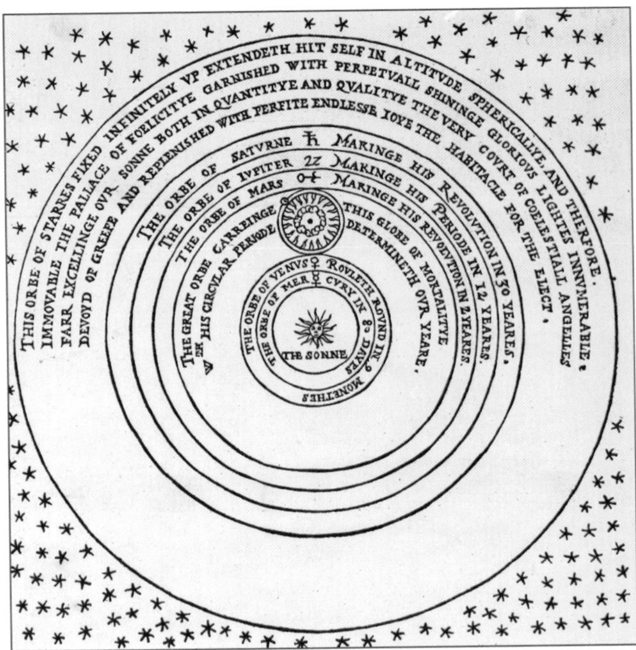

In 1576 Thomas Digges created this diagram of the universe based on the heliocentric theories of Copernicus.

The annual almanac showing the phases of the moon and the relative positions of the moon and the sun were common by 1600. Even today, some farmers plant crops according to the phases of the moon, though there is no scientific evidence that such planting makes any difference in crops. Modern almanacs are much more helpful in giving predictions of weather patterns and soil conditions.

Novel Views

The comfortable, medieval view of the earth as the center of the universe—on which astrology was based—was shattered during the Elizabethan era. A Polish astronomer, Nicolaus Copernicus, had published a book in 1543 arguing that the earth and the planets rotated around the sun. An Englishman, Thomas Digges, went beyond Copernicus and in 1576 theorized that stars really were other suns and that the universe had no boundaries.

Copernicus, Digges, and others who advocated this heliocentric (sun-centered) model had a great impact on fellow scientists, but few outside the scientific community knew the traditional view was being challenged. That changed in 1572, when a new star appeared. It was what now is called a supernova, and it shone so brightly for fourteen months that it was visible even in the daytime. Its appearance, A.L. Rowse writes, "did more to shake Aristotelian [from the Greek philosopher Aristotle] physics and cosmology to ordinary minds than any amount of mathematical demonstration."[82] After all, the stars were supposed to have been fixed for all time by God at the Creation, according to the biblical Book of Genesis. It was not until the following century that the heliocentric view came to be generally accepted, but the supernova was the beginning of the end of astrology as a science.

The widespread belief in astrology extended to medicine. One of England's leading doctors, William Clowes, was a pioneer in the use of mercury to treat syphilis, a cure that, while effective, often poisoned the patient. Clowes believed, however, that signs of the zodiac governed various parts of the body. He would refuse to cut on an arm, for instance, if the sign at that particular time was the one supposedly governing the arm. He wrote, "I judge it very dangerous to touch any part of man's body with lancet or knife whenas the moon hath motion in that sign [of the zodiac] which governeth the part that should be striken."[83]

Indeed, medicine in Elizabethan England was largely medieval mumbo jumbo. Edward Topsell wrote a popular book in which he claimed that the eyes of dragons "being kept till they be stale and afterwards beat into an oil with honey and made into an ointment keep anyone that useth it from the terror of night visions."[84] There were plenty of unscrupulous doctors who claimed to have such ingredients and who sold their potions to trusting patients.

Folk Remedies

Outlandish remedies were common. Powdered armadillo bone was supposed to cure deafness. A dead mouse, cut in half and placed on a wart, was supposed to remove it. Scrofula, a knotty tumor just under the skin, was called "the king's evil" because it supposedly could be cured by a touch of a ruler's hand. Clowes said that such tumors could not be cured by surgery but rather by "a divine and holy curation, which is most admirable to the world, that I have seen and known performed and done by the sacred hands of the Queen's most royal Majesty."[85] The practice continued in England until the 1700s.

Most modern-day medicines were completely unknown. Although a few diseases were treated with chemicals such as

A page from a sixteenth-century manuscript shows some of the natural remedies, including herbs and precious stones, commonly used to treat ailments.

mercury, zinc, and arsenic, these often did more harm than good. Natural treatments, such as herbs, were more popular and sometimes worked, although doctors seldom knew why. Most Elizabethan botanists (scientists who study plants) were also doctors. One, Sir John Salusbury, prescribed this remedy for a backache:

Good sir if you lack the strengthe in
your back
and would have a Remediado
Take Eryngo [ginger] rootes and Marybone tartes
Redd wine and rich Potato
An oyster pie and a Lobsters thigh
hard eggs well dressed in Marrow
This will ease your backes disease
and make you a good Cocksparrowe.
An Apricock or an Artichoke
Anchovies oyle and Pepper
These to use doe not refuse
twill make your back the better.[86]

Medical Tips for Children

In his autobiography, Lord Herbert of Cherbury gave these hints for treating sick children. It shows Elizabethan medicine's reliance on herbs. The passage is found in Elizabethan People: State and Society, *edited by Joel Hurstfield and Alan G.R. Smith.*

And first, I find, that in the infants those diseases are to be remedied which may be hereditary unto them on either side; so that, if they be subject to the [gall]stone or gravel, I do conceive it will be good for the nurse [breast-feeding the baby] sometimes to drink posset drinks, in which are boiled such things as are good to expel gravel and stone; the child also himself when he comes to some age may use the same posset drinks of herbs . . . good for the stone many are reckoned by the physicians, of which also myself could bring a large catalogue, but rather leave it to those who are expert in that art. The same course is to be taken for the gout; for which purpose I do much commend the bathing of children's legs and feet in the water wherein smiths quench their iron, as also water wherein alum hath been infused, or boiled. . . . They that are also subject to the spleen from their ancestors, ought to use those herbs that are splenetics: and those that are troubled with the falling sickness, with cephaniques, of which certainly I should have had need but for the purging of my ears above mentioned. Briefly, what disease soever it be that is derived from ancestors of either side, it will be necessary first to give such medicines to the nurse as may make her milk effectual for those purposes; as also afterwards to give unto the child itself such specific remedies as his age and constitution will bear.

As an allegorical representation of the deadly plague, this sixteenth-century illustration shows English townspeople fleeing from skeletons holding hourglasses.

Little could be done to cure diseases because no one really knew what caused them. Some people blamed the stars when they became ill. Some thought gluttony or drunkenness was the cause. Some blamed England's cold, damp climate. During widespread outbreaks of disease, such as the plague, Jews were accused of poisoning wells. It was not until the invention of the microscope in the next century that scientists could see what caused disease and how it was spread.

The Plague

Doctors were helpless in the face of epidemics. The plague, or Black Death, had first broken out in Europe in the mid-1300s and reappeared frequently. About 20,000 Londoners were killed in 1563 and 30,500 in 1603. Doctors and city officials knew the plague was highly contagious but had no idea how it was spread. They knew the bodies of the dead should be avoided, that their houses should be shut up, and that garbage should be burned. Their orders were mostly ignored. Elizabethan government, Rowse writes, was "insufficiently organised to carry out with success an elaborate set of unpopular orders. . . . The authorities were forced to sit with folded hands until the plague had spent itself."[87]

Instead, the people relied on folk wisdom. They crowded around burial pits at funerals because they believed no one could be infected while attending a religious service. Some treated the plague by holding plucked chickens against the buboes (swelling) to draw out the poison.

Surgery was still extremely primitive. The Royal College of Surgeons had been formed in 1540 by merging the surgeon and barber guilds, and many surgeons were still also barbers. Surgeons, however, were not considered doctors. In fact, they were prohibited from practicing medicine by the rival Royal College of Physicians, which wanted to keep a monopoly on the profession. Still, some advances were made. Frenchman Ambrose Paré developed a method of ligating (sewing shut) stumps after amputation of arms or legs instead of cauterizing (sealing with boiling pitch or a red-hot iron). Paré was wise enough, however, to know the extent of his own ignorance and not to take too much credit. "I treated him," he said, "and God cured him."[88]

Studies in Anatomy

While the greatest strides in medicine lay in the future, some crucial first steps were taken in Elizabeth's time. Perhaps chief among these was a far greater understanding of how the human body was constructed. Most of what doctors knew—or thought they knew—about human anatomy came from the work of the Greek physician Galen (A.D. 129–216), who was prohibited by Roman law from dissecting human bodies and instead inferred human structure from that of dogs and other animals.

Shortly before Elizabeth's reign, however, a Belgian physician, Andreas Vesalius, concluded that much of Galen's assumptions were wrong. After many years of dissecting human corpses, he published a seven-volume illustrated guide to the human body.

Vesalius's work paved the way for William Harvey, the greatest English physician of the Elizabethan era. Studying under Hieronymus Fabricius, who had been a pupil of Vesalius, Harvey observed the pumping action of the heart and the structure of veins, particularly the valves that prevented blood from flowing backward. From such observations and later experiments, Harvey was able to show how blood was pumped by the heart to the lungs to take on oxygen and then to the rest of the body, returning to the heart through the veins. The discovery of circulation of blood would be one of the milestones in medical history.

Mental Illnesses

The Elizabethans also were the first to begin to understand the causes of mental illnesses. Timothy Bright, in his *Treatise of Melancholy* in 1586, suggested that some mental illnesses were caused by "a certain fearful disposition of the mind"[89] and prescribed such things as cheerful music, rest, and a light diet. Previously, doctors thought mental illness was caused by "evil humours" (bodily fluids) that could be reduced by

This sixteenth-century illustration gives some idea how advanced studies in human anatomy had become during Elizabeth's reign.

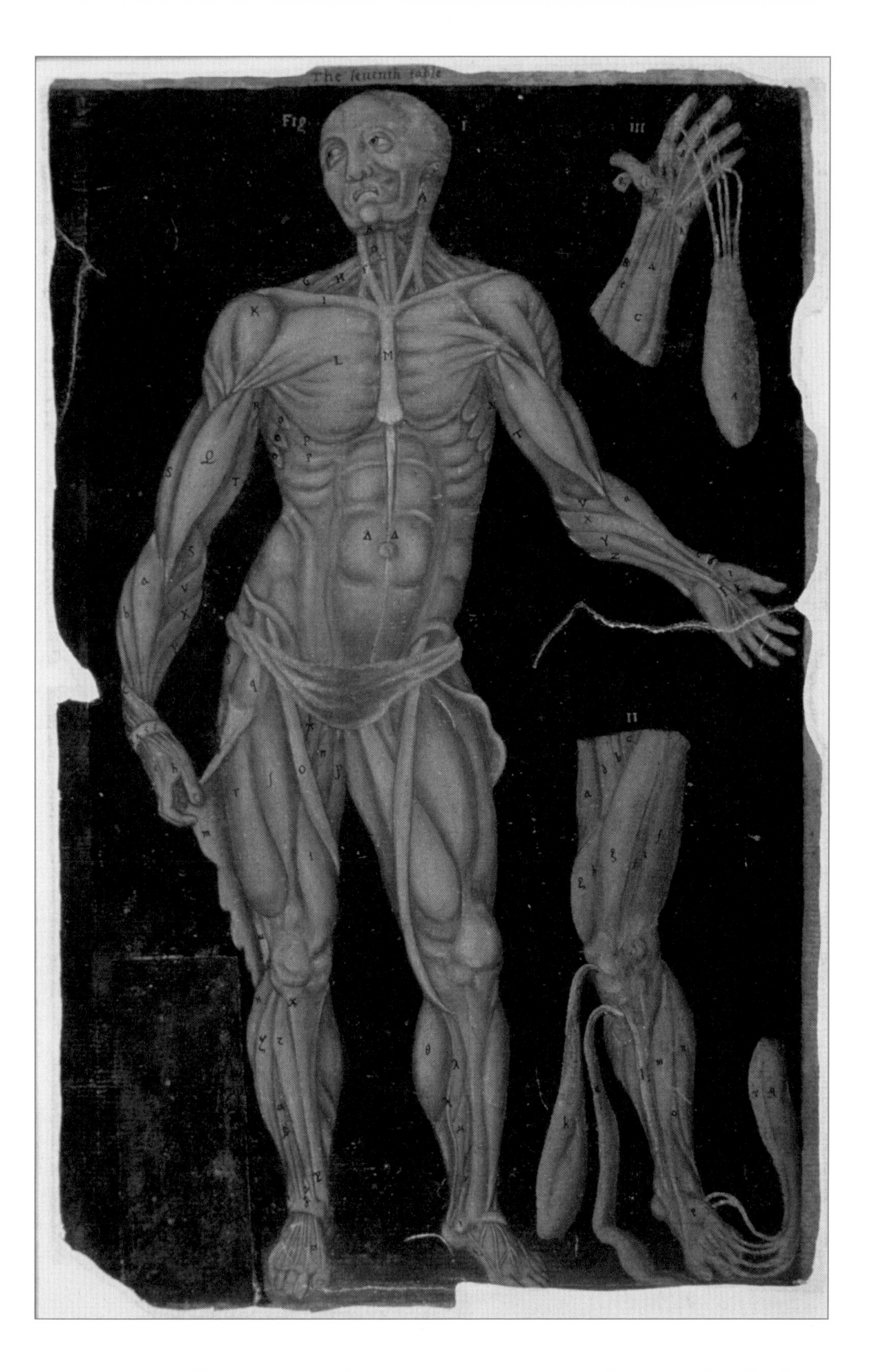
The seventh table
Fig
I
II
III

Thomas Hariot included this illustration as part of his anthropological study of the Native Americans of Virginia.

bloodletting. This treatment consisted of taking blood from a patient by cutting a vein or attaching a bloodsucking leech.

Often, people with mental illnesses were thought to be possessed by devils or, worse, were thought to be the victims of witchcraft. Even university scholars and high church officials believed in witches. Many rural villages had "cunning" women, folk healers who brewed their own medicines, which often proved more effective than those of doctors.

The persecution of witches was never as widespread in England as in the rest of Europe. The English were as superstitious as anyone, but the kind of blind obsession that saw thousands burned at the stake in Germany was foreign to the English character. Thirty persons were hanged for witchcraft in the first twenty years of Elizabeth's reign, but that was a small number compared with the number of those executed for other crimes—forty in 1598 alone from just the county of Somerset.

Many of the great scientific accomplishments of the Elizabethan Age resulted from the exploration of the New World. In 1585, when Sir Walter Raleigh sent his first expedition to colonize North America, he included Thomas Hariot, the first great English anthropologist (one who studies human society). Raleigh wanted Hariot to study not only the plants and animals but also the Native Americans of what would become Virginia. Hariot's book, *Briefe and*

True Report of the New Found Land of Virginia, was the recognized authority for the next century on life in North America. He described native animals and plants, including tobacco, which would soon be popular in England. He learned the language of the natives and wrote about their customs.

Hariot also was a skilled physicist and astronomer and used his knowledge to give Raleigh improved navigational charts and instruments. He invented a new instrument for observing the sun and calculating a ship's position on the sea. He was the first to compile a table that showed how to find due east or due west by observing where the sun rose or set.

Gilbert and Magnetism

William Gilbert was Europe's foremost expert on magnetism. His book *De Magnete,* published in 1600, described for the first time the earth's magnetic field, showing why a compass needle pointed north. He showed how rubbing certain objects, such as amber, made them attract light objects. He called such objects *electriks* and speculated on the force they generated, thus paving the way for the science of electronics. His discoveries led to vast improvements in compasses and other navigational instruments. His work also was a major influence on Sir Isaac Newton, who, in another century, would propose the law of gravity.

Perhaps the greatest scientific achievement of the Elizabethan Age, however, was not a single discovery. The man behind it, Francis Bacon, was known more as a philosopher and a politician than as a scientist. His contribution was to the theory

The Medical Profession

In his Advancement of Learning, *written in 1605, Francis Bacon discusses what he believes to be the poor state of the medical profession. His criticism is reprinted in* Elizabethan People: State and Society, *edited by Joel Hurstfield and Alan G.R. Smith.*

"Nay, we see the weakness and credulity of men is such, as they will often prefer a mountebank or witch before a learned physician. . . . And what followeth? Even this, that physicians say to themselves, as Solomon expresseth it upon a higher occasion: 'If it befal me as befalleth to the fools, why should I labour to be more wise?' And therefore I cannot much blame physicians that they use commonly to intend some other art or practice, which they fancy, more than their profession. For you shall have them antiquaries, poets, humanists, statesmen, merchants, divines, and in every of these better seen than in their profession; and no doubt upon this ground, that they find that mediocrity and excellency in their art maketh no difference in profit or reputation toward their fortune. . . . Medicine is a science which hath been (as we have said) more professed than laboured, and yet more laboured than advanced; the labour having been, in my judgment, rather in circle than in progression. For I find much iteration, but small addition."

of science. The accepted method of scientific investigation had been to form a theory and then try to prove it. Bacon said, instead, that knowledge can come only from experimentation and observation of facts. He said that instead of being *deductive*—starting with a general assumption and working down to specifics—science should be *inductive*—arriving at a general conclusion based on observations.

Bacon was one of the first persons in history to combine science with philosophy. He argued that humanity—not nature—is the primary shaper of events and that it is up to people, through observation and experiments, to use nature to make life on earth better. He recognized that science is not a set of disconnected discoveries, but that each sets the stage for another. He wrote that the important part of history is not wars or conquests but the development of ideas and thought.

Defending Criticism

Bacon was criticized by clergymen who claimed that men should not seek to unravel what God meant to be a mystery. He replied that it was God who had enabled humans to better understand the world around them:

> We see that God vouchsafeth to descend to the weakness of our capacity, so expressing and unfolding His Mysteries as they may be best comprehended by us; and inoculate, as it were, His Revelations upon the conceptions and notions of our Reason; and so applying His inspirations to open our understandings, as the form of the key is fitted to the ward of the lock. In which respect notwithstanding, we ought not to be wanting to our selves; for seeing God makes use of the faculty and function of Reason in His Illuminations, we ought also every way to employ and improve the same, whereby we may become more capable to receive and draw in such Holy Mysteries.[90]

Bacon's view of inductive, or experimental, science quickly became popular. It did not eventually become the prevailing procedure; deductive science remains the preferred method of discovery. His concept, however, greatly influenced the experimental scientists of the next century, including the astronomer Galileo.

Bacon's writings also led a group of scientists to begin holding meetings to discuss their experiments. This group eventually became the world's most famous scientific organization, the Royal Society. The author of the first published history of the society wrote that Bacon was "the one great man, who had the true imagination of the whole extent of this enterprise, as it is now set on foot."[91]

Chapter Seven

Toward the New World

When England finally joined its European neighbors in the exploration of the New World, more than half a century had passed since Christopher Columbus's 1492 voyage. The English made up for their late start with the boldness that marked the age. By the end of Elizabeth's reign, England was the world's leading sea power, was firmly established in North America, and had laid the foundations of the British Empire.

England's success was attributable to the intense interest of the country's leaders—including Elizabeth—in the profits to be made by the incredible bravery and spirit of its sailors. "What shall we be?" Sir Walter Raleigh asked, "Travelers or tinkers; conquerors or novices?"[92]

Elizabeth's sailors endured terrible hardships and dangers. When they ran short of food on voyages (which was often), they ate everything except one another—including penguins on the southern tip of South America and polar bears in the Arctic. Their exploits began the legend of English sea power, which was to reach a peak with the defeat of the great Spanish fleet, the Armada, in 1588.

Elizabeth's grandfather, Henry VII, made only a small attempt to explore the Americas. In 1497 he sent an English sea captain, John Cabot, on a voyage to what is now Greenland, Nova Scotia, and Newfoundland. Cabot was looking both for riches and for the Northwest Passage, a way around America into the Pacific Ocean. He found neither, and Henry soon lost interest.

The Start of Exploration

While Elizabeth's father, Henry VIII, was feuding with the pope about his divorce, Spain conquered Mexico and Peru, and Portugal founded colonies in India and the Philippines. The real start of English exploration and trade came with the reign of Elizabeth's brother, Edward VI. Hugh

Willoughby and Richard Chancellor led an expedition in 1553 that went around Scandinavia to the north to try to find a northeast passage to Asia. The expedition failed to find any passage, but it opened trade between England and Russia.

The other focus of English activity was West Africa, which supposedly was the exclusive territory of Portugal. In 1493 Pope Alexander VI had divided the unknown lands of Africa and the Americas between Spain and Portugal. This, however, did not stop the sailors of Protestant England. Thomas Windham began trading on the Barbary and Gold Coasts in the early 1550s. Another early explorer, Richard Hakluyt, wrote that the Portuguese "were much offended with this our new trade into Barbary . . . and gave out that if they took us in those parts, they would use us as their mortal enemies."[93]

Henry VIII did, however, make a lasting contribution to England's eventual naval prowess and the subsequent opportunities for overseas expansion. Although England was not strong enough to challenge Spain's grip on the Americas, Henry could see that the future of trade lay across the Atlantic and that ships carrying rich cargos would have to be defended. Accordingly, he founded the Royal Navy.

Not only did Henry order the royal dockyards to build a fleet of fighting ships, but they were ships the like of which Europe had not seen since the days of the Viking longboats. Instead of the clumsy, rounded tubs normally used for sea voyages, the new English ships were "race built." That is, they were much longer in comparison to their width and thus were able to slice through the rougher Atlantic waves. Gone were the high, bulky forecastles and hindcastles—useful in carrying archers in close Mediterranean battles but rendering ships less maneuverable in stronger Atlantic winds.

The new ships had better fighting abilities as well. The days when ramming and boarding would decide sea battles was over. Gunnery was the way of the future, and Henry's designers took the bold step of placing guns below decks, ready to be deployed through ports, or windows in the hull, to deliver the dreaded broadside.

John Hawkins

Such heroics, however, lay in the future. The first great voyages under Elizabeth were those of John Hawkins. Hawkins, whose father had also been a sea captain, knew that the Spanish in the New World needed labor for their plantations. He sailed to Guinea in 1562, bought or captured about three hundred Africans, and sailed to the West Indies, where he sold them as slaves. The trip was so profitable that Elizabeth herself invested in his next one, which was just as much a moneymaker.

By the time Hawkins made his third voyage, however, King Philip of Spain no longer wanted Englishmen in his domains. In 1568 Hawkins's ships were at San Juan de Ulloa when a large Spanish fleet appeared at the mouth of the Mexican harbor. Rather than

This is a replica of the Golden Hind, *the ship captained by Sir Francis Drake as he circumnavigated the globe.*

exchange gunfire with Hawkins, the Spanish commander signaled that the English would be allowed to leave. Then, when the Spaniards were close enough, they rushed and boarded the English ships. Only two ships escaped—the *Minion,* with Hawkins in command, and the *Judith,* commanded by one of Hawkins's best young captains, Francis Drake.

San Juan de Ulloa ended the friendship that had existed between England and Spain since the previous century. Not only did England think its ships had been taken by treachery, but many of the captured sailors were harshly treated. Some were burned at the stake for their Protestant beliefs. A.L. Rowse writes, "One must not . . . underestimate the force of the hatred for Spain all this piled up among the Protestants of Europe."[94]

Elizabeth wanted revenge, and she wanted more profits from America, but she did not want war with Spain. She promised Philip that English adventures in America would stop, but she secretly encouraged them. The result was a decade of undeclared war on Spain by English privateers—mainly Drake.

A Lion at Sea

English explorers encountered all sorts of unfamiliar animals. This "lion" described by Edward Hare, who sailed with Sir Humphrey Gilbert to Newfoundland, was probably a walrus. The description is found in The Horizon Book of the Elizabethan World *by Lacey Baldwin Smith, edited by Norman Kotler.*

So upon Saturday in the afternoon of the thirty-first of August, we changed our course and returned back for England, at which very instant, even in winding about, there passed along between us and toward the land which we now forsook a very lion to our seeming, in shape, hair, and color, not swimming after the manner of a beast by moving of his feet, but rather sliding upon the water with his whole body (excepting the legs) in sight, neither yet diving under and again rising above the water, as the manner is of whales, dolphines, tunnies [tuna], porpoises, and all other fish, but confidently showing himself above water without hiding; notwithstanding, we presented ourselves in open view and gesture to amaze him, as all creatures will be commonly at a sudden gaze and sight of men. Thus he passed along turning his head to and fro, yawning and gaping wide, with ugly demonstration of long teeth and glaring eyes, and to bid us a farewell (coming tight against the *Hind* [the *Golden Hind,* Gilbert's ship]) he sent forth a horrible voice, roaring or bellowing as doth a lion, which spectacle we all beheld so far as we were able to discern the same, as men prone to wonder at every strange thing, as this doubtless was, to see a lion in the ocean sea, or fish in shape of a lion.

Drake was one of the outstanding figures, not only of the Elizabethan Age but in all English history as well. He was the most famous of Elizabeth's subjects, loved by the English for his boldness and feared by the Spanish, who called him "El Draque" (the Dragon). Englishmen loved to tell about his raiding of the Spanish harbor of Cádiz in 1587 and "singeing of the King of Spain's beard,"[95] as the popular saying went. The story goes that Drake was bowling when informed that the Spanish Armada had been sighted off Plymouth in England. "We have time to finish the game and beat the Spaniards, too,"[96] he is supposed to have said. It was Drake who gave the English their reputation as being unconquerable at sea.

Sir John Hawkins made a small fortune selling African slaves to the Spanish in the New World.

Drake in the Caribbean

Drake's first voyage, in 1571, was mainly to look over Spanish territory in the Caribbean to find the likeliest targets. On his second voyage, in 1572–1573, he captured the town of Nombre de Dios in Panama and made off with forty thousand pounds in gold and silver from Spanish mines in Peru. When he arrived back in Plymouth on a Sunday morning, word spread throughout the city, even into St. Andrew's Church. The people were so filled "with desire and delight to see him," writes naval historian J.S. Corbett, "that very few or none remained with the preacher."[97]

While in Panama, Drake had climbed a high tree from which he could see the Pacific Ocean and prayed that he might someday sail those waters. Elizabeth had refused others permission to raid Spanish possessions on America's western coast, but in 1577 she approved Drake's plan to conduct such a raid, saying, "Drake! So it is that I would gladly be revenged on the King of Spain for divers injuries that I have received."[98]

Drake's Pacific voyage had plenty of backers, including Elizabeth, Leicester, Hawkins, and Elizabeth's secretary of state, Francis Walsingham. When rumors of the expedition reached Spain and

Francis Drake's Voyage Around the World

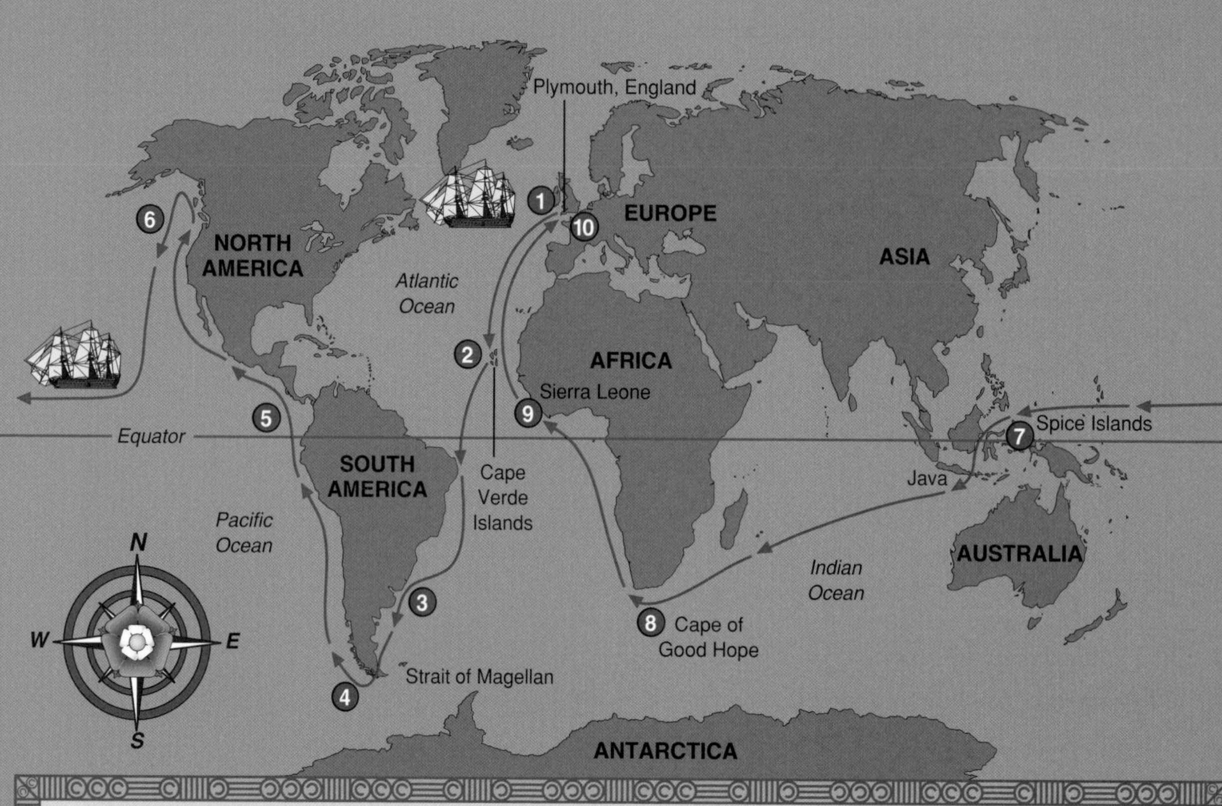

1. Francis Drake departs Plymouth, England, on December 13, 1577, with 160 men and three large ships: the *Pelican*, the *Elizabeth*, and the *Marigold*, plus two additional supply ships.

2. Drake captures a Portuguese ship encountered in the Cape Verde Islands.

3. After the expedition stops for supplies, the supply ships and Portuguese ship are abandoned. Captain Thomas Doughty is executed for mutiny. Drake renames the *Pelican* the *Golden Hind* (deer).

4. Violent storms wreck the *Marigold* on the voyage through the Strait of Magellan. The *Elizabeth* is blown off course, becomes lost, and returns to England. Drake and the *Golden Hind* successfully navigate through to the Pacific Ocean.

5. Drake raids Spanish settlements and ships on South America's and Mexico's Pacific shores, collecting gold, silver, jewels, and other precious cargo.

6. The *Golden Hind* sails up the coast of North America, as far as Vancouver or perhaps even Alaska.

7. Trade relations are established with the Spice Islands and 6 tons of cloves are taken aboard.

8. Drake sails around the Cape of Good Hope at the southern tip of Africa.

9. The ship anchors in Sierra Leone, its first stop since leaving the Indonesian island of Java.

10. On September 26, 1580, Drake and his men sail into Plymouth Harbor on a ship loaded with treasure from around the world. Queen Elizabeth visits Drake on board the *Golden Hind* and grants him knighthood.

Philip complained, Elizabeth wrote him personally, saying, "We beg very affectionately that all suspicions may be banished from between us, if any such have been raised by the acts of wicked men with the object of destroying the close friendship which we enjoyed in our earlier years."[99]

The voyage, begun in 1577, had all the elements of an adventure yarn—violent storms at sea, shortages of food, even an unsuccessful mutiny. Of his three ships, only Drake's flagship, the *Pelican,* made it through the Strait of Magellan at the tip of South America. Drake renamed his ship the *Golden Hind* (deer), the symbol of one of his chief sponsors, Lord Hatton, and began attacking the unsuspecting and undefended Spanish settlements along the coasts of Chile and Peru and capturing Spanish ships.

Drake's objective was plunder, not punishment. He did not kill Spaniards unless attacked, and he treated prisoners graciously. One Spanish captain gave this account:

> When our ship was sacked, no [English] man dared take anything without his orders: he shows them great favour, but punishes the least fault. . . . Each one takes particular pains to keep his arquebus [a type of gun] clean. He also carried painters who paint for him pictures of the coast in exact colours. He carried trained carpenters and artisans, so as to be able to careen the ship at any time. . . . He is served on silver dishes with gold borders and gilded garlands. . . . He dines and sups to the music of viols.[100]

Sir Francis Drake plundered several Spanish settlements in South America during his voyage around the world.

Return to England

Drake continued up the coast, then crossed the Pacific and sailed around India and Africa and back to England. He arrived in Plymouth after a voyage of thirty-four months. His first question on entering the harbor was whether Elizabeth was alive and well. Indeed she was, and she was pleased with Drake for his exploits and even more pleased with the treasure he brought her. She even went to visit him on the *Golden Hind.* When he knelt before her, she joked that she had a sword ready to cut off his head. Instead, she made him a knight.

Elizabeth knights Francis Drake in recognition of his extraordinary achievement of circumnavigating the globe.

When the Spanish ambassador demanded that Drake be brought to trial for piracy and the treasure returned, Elizabeth claimed not to know what he was talking about.

Drake's voyage around the world and his success against the supposedly all-powerful Spanish raised the world's opinion of England. More important, it raised England's opinion of itself. Hakluyt, whose account of Elizabethan explorations was published in 1589, boasted:

What ever ships did heretofore . . . pass and repass the unpassable (in former opinion) strait of Magellan, range along the coast of Chile, Peru and all the backside of nova Hispania, further than any Christian ever passed, traverse the mighty breadth of the South Sea . . . and traffic with the princes of the Moluccas . . . and last of all return home most richly laden with the commodities of China, as the subjects of this now flourishing monarchy have done?[101]

Ironically, much of Drake's Spanish treasure went to help the Dutch, who were rebelling against their Spanish overlords. His adventures made war between England and Spain almost inevitable, particularly after the execution of Mary, Queen of Scots, in 1587 put an end to her plotting against Elizabeth. As her brother-in-law, King Charles IX of France, had predicted, "Ah! The poor fool will never cease until she loses her head."[102]

The Spanish Armada

King Philip of Spain's dreams of conquering England, however, would vanish along with most of his vaunted fleet, the Spanish Armada. Though vastly superior in numbers to the English, the Spanish could not match their rivals either in sailing or gunnery, all the legacy of Elizabeth's father.

The defeat of the Armada was a major turning point in world history. Spain was the strongest nation in Europe, and the Armada had been considered the finest, most powerful fleet ever assembled. Its defeat marked the beginning of Spain's

The New World Learns About Elizabeth

Elizabeth was praised far and wide, even in the New World, as this passage from The Discovery of Guiana *by Sir Walter Raleigh shows. It is found in* The Horizon Book of the Elizabethan World *by Lacey Baldwin Smith, edited by Norman Kotler.*

We then hastened away toward our purposed discovery, and first I called all the captains [native chiefs] of the islands together that were enemies to the Spaniards, for there were some which Berrio [a Spanish official] had brought out of other countries and planted there to eat out and waste those that were natural of the place, and by my Indian interpreter, which I carried out of England, I made them understand that I was the servant of a queen, who was the great cacique [chief] of the north, and a virgin and had more caciques under her than there were trees in that island: that she was an enemy to the Castelani [Spaniards] to respect of their tyranny and oppression, and that she delivered all such nations about her as were by them oppressed, and having freed all the coast of the northern world from their servitude had sent me to free them also, and with all to defend the country of Guiana from their invasion and conquest. I showed them Her Majesty's picture, which they so admired and honored, as it had been easy to have brought them idolatrous thereof.

long decline as a world power. Spain still was powerful, but the peak of Spanish might had passed.

The defeat of the Armada also was a blow to the Roman Catholic Church. First, it ensured that England would remain Protestant. There would be no more serious attempts to return the English church to the pope's rule. Second, it weakened Spain to the point where the Netherlands were able to shake off Spanish domination, thus enabling the Protestant Dutch to stay independent of the Catholic Church.

For England, however, the victory was the start of a rise to prominence. The island nation, which had been lightly regarded by the rest of Europe, was now considered a power to be reckoned with. Also, with the threat of invasion removed, England could begin her own program of colonization in the Americas and elsewhere—a program that would lead eventually to the establishment of the British Empire.

Just as important, the victory created a spirit of national pride and confidence among the English. With this spirit came a burst of creativity in science, literature, and drama. While the Elizabethan Age began with the young queen's coronation, most of the greatest achievements—Shakespeare's plays, the colonization of North America—were packed into the two decades following the defeat of the Armada.

The English navy and the Spanish Armada exchange cannon fire in a fierce battle. The defeat of the Armada established England as a powerful force in European politics.

In the Americas

In 1584 Sir Walter Raleigh received a charter from Elizabeth empowering him "to discover barbarous countries, not actually possessed of any Christian prince and inhabited by Christian people, to occupy and enjoy the same for ever."[103] The next year an expedition commanded by Raleigh's cousin, Sir Richard Grenville, established a colony of one hundred men on Roanoke Island, off the coast of what Raleigh named Virginia, in honor of Elizabeth, the "Virgin Queen."

The first Roanoke colony lasted only a year because of a lack of supplies. Most of the colonists returned to England, leaving behind only fifteen men. Raleigh reestablished the colony in 1587, this time bringing seventeen women along with one hundred men. The inclusion of women showed that England's goal was a permanent settlement, an extension of England itself, rather than a trading post.

Because of the war with Spain, supply ships were not sent to Roanoke until 1590. The colonists had disappeared, probably massacred by Indians. Ever since, Roanoke has been known as the Lost Colony. The English were so disappointed that no new settlement was attempted until after Elizabeth's death, when permanent colonies were founded at Jamestown in Virginia (1607) and in Guiana in South America (1609).

The start of English colonization was the beginning of the British Empire. The colonies themselves were established under Elizabeth's successors, but they had been made possible only by the grand spirit of exploration and adventure that was part of the Elizabethan era. England's colonies would be far different from those of other European countries. As Lacey Baldwin Smith writes:

> Of the imperial powers, only England succeeded in transplanting its people and establishing small, tough, and vital replicas of itself on the inhospitable shores and in the endless forests of an uncharted land. . . . Only England sent out viable offshoots with men to toil, women to be fruitful, children to endure the future, and laws by which to live.[104]

Epilogue

A Living Legacy

In many ways, the Elizabethan era never ended. Its achievements have echoed through the centuries. Much of the world owes basic elements of language, law, and religion to the Elizabethans. As A.L. Rowse writes, "The Elizabethan Age is not something dead and apart from us: it is alive and all round us and within us . . . part of our living experience, entering into our conscious tradition and into the secret channels of heart and blood."[105]

One of the greatest contributions of Elizabethan England is the English language itself. A prominent linguist once wrote that "no other half century has done so much for the permanent enrichment of the language as that which is covered by Shakespeare's lifetime."[106] The credit for this goes to the Elizabethan writers. Of these, Shakespeare towers above all the rest. It is doubtful that any writer in history better captured the soul of his language and of his people. Not only the language, but also the feeling of Elizabethan England, comes to us through his plays and poetry. As one scholar says, "It is astonishing how little out of touch with Shakespeare and his age we are. . . . We have changed in the things we *do;* but how little yet have those things changed us in what we *are.*"[107]

The Queen and Her Church

Of all the accomplishments of the Elizabethan Age, one is due mostly to the queen personally—the Church of England. She rejected the Catholic Church but would not allow the Puritans and other reformers to go too far. Rowse writes that she "gave the English Church [a] chance to take root, to grow into the minds and hearts of later generations."[108] Every bride or groom who has repeated the vows "for better, for worse, for richer, for poorer, in sickness and health,

The reign of Queen Elizabeth is remembered today as a time of exceptional prosperity and cultural achievement.

to love and to cherish, till death us do part" can thank Elizabeth, who ensured the survival of the Church of England prayer book containing the famous vow.

The entire Elizabethan experience—religion, language, drama—would not have spread so far and so fast had it not been for the great burst of exploration and colonization. Rowse writes, "The English entered late, but in the end most effectively of all—and that was the work of the Elizabethans. . . . They foreshadowed the ways their people were to take in the centuries to come."[109] England's concept of law and its representative form of government, as well as its language and religion, were carried everywhere from America to India.

The Elizabethan era has inspired not only the English but also people throughout the world—Americans, Indians, Africans, Canadians, Jamaicans, Egyptians—people everywhere who, at one time or another, were part of the British Empire. Many British colonies, such as the United States, went their own ways. Yet they owe much of their culture to Elizabeth's England. It was, as Muriel St. Clair Byrne writes, "one of those rare periods when the past and the future are both coloured by imagination, and both shed a glory on the present."[110]

Notes

Introduction: The Golden Days

1. Quoted in Carolly Erickson, *The First Elizabeth.* New York: Summit, 1983, p. 167.
2. A.H. Dodd, *Elizabethan England.* New York: G.P. Putnam's Sons, 1973, p. 15.
3. Quoted in Erickson, *The First Elizabeth,* p. 167.

Chapter One: Gloriana and Her Reign

4. Quoted in Susan Watkins, *In Public and Private: Elizabeth I and Her World.* New York: Thames and Hudson, 1998, p. 149.
5. Quoted in Erickson, *The First Elizabeth,* p. 20.
6. Quoted in Elizabeth Jenkins, *Elizabeth the Great.* New York: Capricorn, 1958, p. 60.
7. Quoted in Mary M. Luke, *Gloriana: The Years of Elizabeth I.* New York: Coward, McCann & Geoghegan, 1973, p. 32.
8. Quoted in Erickson, *The First Elizabeth,* p. 179.
9. Quoted in Lisa Hopkins, *Queen Elizabeth I and Her Court.* London: Vision, 1990, p. 137.
10. Quoted in Luke, *Gloriana,* p. 36.
11. Quoted in Erickson, *The First Elizabeth,* p. 178.
12. Erickson, *The First Elizabeth,* p. 251.
13. Quoted in Edith Sitwell, *The Queens and the Hive.* Boston: Little, Brown, 1962, p. 48.
14. Quoted in Milton Waldman, *Rod of Iron.* Boston: Houghton Mifflin, 1941, p. 154.
15. Quoted in Susan Watkins, *In Public and Private,* p. 164.
16. Quoted in Ralph Dutton, *English Court Life from Henry VII to George II.* London: B.T. Batsford, 1963, p. 66.
17. Quoted in Muriel St. Clair Byrne, *Elizabethan Life in Town and Country.* London: Methuen, 1961, p. 20.
18. Quoted in S.T. Bindoff, *Tudor England.* Baltimore: Penguin, 1950, p. 306.
19. Quoted in Byrne, *Elizabethan Life in Town and Country,* p. 21.
20. Quoted in Byrne, *Elizabethan Life in Town and Country,* p. 23.

Chapter Two: The Queen Bee and Her Hive

21. Quoted in Alfred L. Rowse and George B. Harrison, *Queen Elizabeth and Her Subjects.* Freeport, NY: Books for Libraries, 1935, p. 96.
22. Quoted in Alfred L. Rowse, *The Elizabethan Renaissance: The Life of the Society.* New York: Charles Scribner's Sons, 1971, p. 56.
23. Quoted in Erickson, *The First Elizabeth,* p. 230.

24. Quoted in Rowse, *The Elizabethan Renaissance: The Life of the Society*, p. 31.
25. Quoted in Peter Brimacombe, *All the Queen's Men: The World of Elizabeth I.* New York: St. Martin's, 2000, p. 48.
26. Quoted in Ian Dunlop, *Palaces and Progresses of Elizabeth I.* New York: Taplinger, 1970, p. 23.
27. Quoted in Mary Hill Cole, *The Portable Queen: Elizabeth I and the Politics of Ceremony.* Amherst: University of Massachusetts Press, 1999, p. 65.
28. Quoted in Dunlop, *Palaces and Progresses of Elizabeth I*, p. 151.
29. Christopher Morris, *The Tudors*, Glasgow: Fontana Collins, 1966, p. 137.
30. Quoted in Rachel and Allen Percival, *The Court of Elizabeth the First.* London: Stainer and Bell, 1976, p. 75.
31. Rowse, *The Elizabethan Renaissance: The Life of the Society*, p. 30.

Chapter Three: London and the Cities

32. Quoted in Alfred L. Rowse, *The England of Elizabeth.* Madison: University of Wisconsin Press, 1978, p. 109.
33. Rowse, *The England of Elizabeth*, p. 160.
34. Quoted in Robert Gray, *A History of London.* New York: Taplinger, 1979, p. 142.
35. Quoted in Gray, *A History of London*, p. 145.
36. Quoted in Byrne, *Elizabethan Life in Town and Country*, p. 80.
37. Quoted in Byrne, *Elizabethan Life in Town and Country*, p. 83.
38. Quoted in Rowse, *The Elizabethan Renaissance: The Life of the Society*, p. 158.
39. Quoted in Byrne, *Elizabethan Life in Town and Country*, p. 103.
40. Quoted in Gray, *A History of London*, p. 139.
41. Quoted in Gray, *A History of London*, p. 143.
42. Quoted in Byrne, *Elizabethan Life in Town and Country*, p. 92
43. Quoted in Byrne, *Elizabethan Life in Town and Country*, p. 86.
44. Quoted in Byrne, *Elizabethan Life in Town and Country*, p. 98.
45. Quoted in Gray, *A History of London*, p. 139.
46. Quoted in Dodd, *Elizabethan England*, p. 67.
47. Rowse, *The England of Elizabeth*, p. 164.

Chapter Four: The Question of Faith

48. Quoted in Rowse, *The England of Elizabeth*, p. 397.
49. Quoted in Rowse, *The England of Elizabeth*, p. 387.
50. Quoted in Morris, *The Tudors*, p. 159.
51. Bindoff, *Tudor England*, p. 224.
52. Quoted in Morris, *The Tudors*, p. 159.
53. Quoted in Rowse, *The England of Elizabeth*, p. 478.
54. Quoted in Morris, *The Tudors*, p. 160.
55. Quoted in Dutton, *English Court Life from Henry VII to George II*, p. 86.
56. Quoted in Dutton, *English Court Life from Henry VII to George II*, p. 86.
57. Rowse, *The England of Elizabeth*, p. 390.
58. Quoted in Lacey Baldwin Smith, *The Elizabethan World.* Boston: Houghton Mifflin, 1967, p. 173.
59. Quoted in Bindoff, *Tudor England*, p. 238.
60. Quoted in Duncan Harrington, trans., "Two Entries from the Register of Archbishop John Whitgift, Lambeth Palace Library," Crandall Family Association, 2001. www.cfa.net/cfa/lambeth2.html.

Chapter Five: The Country at Play

61. Quoted in Rowse, *The Elizabethan Renaissance: The Life of the Society*, p. 221.
62. Quoted in Rowse, *The Elizabethan Renaissance: The Life of the Society*, p. 204.
63. Quoted in Rowse, *The Elizabethan Renaissance: The Life of the Society*, p. 207
64. Quoted in Rowse, *The Elizabethan Renaissance: The Life of the Society*, p. 214.
65. Byrne, *Elizabethan Life in Town and Country*, p. 241.
66. Quoted in Byrne, *Elizabethan Life in Town and Country*, p. 241.
67. Quoted in Rowse, *The Elizabethan Renaissance: The Life of the Society*, p. 221.
68. Quoted in Rowse, *The Elizabethan Renaissance: The Life of the Society*, p. 144.
69. Quoted in Erickson, *The First Elizabeth*, p. 210.
70. Quoted in Brimacombe, *All the Queen's Men*, p. 48.
71. Quoted in Brimacombe, *All the Queen's Men*, p. 179.
72. Quoted in John Southworth, *Fools and Jesters at the English Court*. Thrupp, England: Sutton, 1998, p. 116.
73. Quoted in Dunlop, *Palaces and Progresses of Elizabeth I*, p. 148.
74. Quoted in Violet Wilson, *Queen Elizabeth's Maids of Honour*. London: John Lane, 1922, p. 79.
75. Quoted in Byrne, *Elizabethan Life in Town and Country*, p. 247.
76. Quoted in Byrne, *Elizabethan Life in Town and Country*, p. 253.

Chapter Six: Science, Medicine, and Superstition

77. Alfred L. Rowse, *The Elizabethan Renaissance: The Cultural Achievement*. New York: Charles Scribner's Sons, 1972, p. 284.
78. Smith, *The Elizabethan World*, p. 251.
79. Quoted in J.J. O'Connor and E.F. Robertson, "John Dee," Turnbull www server, August 2002. http://turnbull.mcs.st-and.ac.uk/~history/Mathematicians/Dee.html.
80. Quoted in Rowse, *The Elizabethan Renaissance: The Life of the Society*, p. 261.
81. Quoted in Rowse, *The Elizabethan Renaissance: The Life of the Society*, p. 260.
82. Rowse, *The Elizabethan Renaissance: The Cultural Achievement*, p. 229.
83. Quoted in Rowse, *The Elizabethan Renaissance: The Cultural Achievement*, p. 288.
84. Quoted in Byrne, *Elizabethan Life in Town and Country*, p. 284.
85. Quoted in Rowse, *The Elizabethan Renaissance: The Cultural Achievement*, p. 291.
86. Quoted in Rowse, *The Elizabethan Renaissance: The Cultural Achievement*, p. 269.
87. Rowse, *The Elizabethan Renaissance: The Cultural Achievement*, p. 282.
88. Quoted in Smith, *The Elizabethan World*, p. 51.
89. Quoted in Rowse, *The Elizabethan Renaissance: The Cultural Achievement*, p. 293.
90. Quoted in Sir Francis Bacon's New Advancement of Learning, "Quotes of Francis Bacon." www.sirbacon.org/links/baconquotes.html.
91. Quoted in Rowse, *The Elizabethan Renaissance: The Cultural Achievement*, p. 262.

Chapter Seven: Toward the New World

92. Quoted in Smith, *The Elizabethan World*, p. 240.

93. Quoted in Alfred L. Rowse, *The Expansion of Elizabethan England.* New York: St. Martin's, 1955, p. 173.
94. Rowse, *The Expansion of Elizabethan England,* p. 176.
95. Quoted in Bindoff, *Tudor England,* p. 255.
96. Quoted in Garrett Mattingly, *The Armada.* Boston: Houghton Mifflin, 1959, p. 265.
97. Quoted in Rowse, *The Expansion of Elizabethan England,* p. 178.
98. Quoted in Rowse, *The Expansion of Elizabethan England,* p. 182.
99. Quoted in Rowse, *The Expansion of Elizabethan England,* p. 182.
100. Quoted in Rowse, *The Expansion of Elizabethan England,* p. 185.
101. Quoted in Rowse, *The Expansion of Elizabethan England,* p. 162
102. Quoted in Smith, *The Elizabethan World,* p. 176.
103. Quoted in Smith, *The Elizabethan World,* p. 244.
104. Smith, *The Elizabethan World,* p. 243.

Epilogue: A Living Legacy

105. Rowse, *The England of Elizabeth,* p. 1.
106. Quoted in Rowse, *The England of Elizabeth,* p. 23.
107. Quoted in Byrne, *Elizabethan Life in Town and Country,* p. 14.
108. Rowse, *The England of Elizabeth,* p. 18.
109. Rowse, *The England of Elizabeth,* p. 29.
110. Byrne, *Elizabethan Life in Town and Country,* p. 1.

For Further Reading

Books

Kathy Elgin, *Elizabethan England.* New York: Facts On File, 2005. A lively study of the fashions and costumes of the Elizabethan era, from typical peasant dress to military uniforms to the elaborate gowns, wigs, and makeup of the queen's court.

Paul Hilliam, *Elizabeth I: Queen of England's Golden Age.* New York: Rosen, 2004. A clearly written biography of England's Renaissance queen that emphasizes her influence on the artists, scholars, and other rulers of the age.

Joy Paige, *Sir Francis Drake: Circumnavigator of the Globe and Privateer for Queen Elizabeth.* New York: Rosen, 2002. A biography of the greatest English explorer of the Elizabethan era, loved and admired by the English for his daring and skill as a raider on the high seas and hated by the Spaniards for the same reasons.

Liza Picard, *Elizabeth's London: Everyday Life in Elizabethan London.* New York: St. Martin's, 2004. This guided tour of sixteenth-century London includes sections on architecture, education, crime and punishment, amusements, medicine, food, and religion. A useful appendix explains Elizabethan words and pronunciations, and the text is supported by dozens of color photographs and maps.

Jane Resh Thomas, *Behind the Mask: The Life of Queen Elizabeth I.* New York: Clarion, 1998. A brightly written biography for young readers, amply illustrated in both color and black and white. The chronology and brief descriptions of major characters are helpful.

Diane Yancey, *Life in the Elizabethan Theater.* San Diego: Lucent, 1996. A colorful study of the playwrights, playhouses, and performances of Elizabethan England, the golden age of Shakespeare, Jonson, and Marlowe, enhanced by primary-source quotations and abundant black-and-white illustrations.

Web Sites

The Life and Times of Queen Elizabeth I (www.elizabethi.org). This comprehensive site details many facets of Elizabeth's life and reign. It includes a "who's who" section, a bibliography, and even a guide to portrayals of Elizabeth in films and on television.

The Official Web Site of the British Monarchy (www.royal.gov.uk). In addition to short biographies of kings and queens dating from 757 to the present, this fascinating site gives information on members of the present royal family and the role of the monarchy, plus pictures of royal residences and art treasures.

Works Consulted

Books

S.T. Bindoff, *Tudor England.* Baltimore: Penguin, 1950. Part of the Pelican History of England series, this volume covers the period from 1485 to 1603. A good, general summary somewhat hampered by the lack of footnotes and a bibliography.

Peter Brimacombe, *All the Queen's Men: The World of Elizabeth I.* New York: St. Martin's, 2000. This work offers biographical information on the many men who played prominent roles during the reign. Not only courtiers but also explorers, scientists, and writers are covered.

Muriel St. Clair Byrne, *Elizabethan Life in Town and Country.* London: Methuen, 1961. A close and personal look at the lives of everyday Englishmen, great and small, during Elizabeth's reign. Ample use of contemporary quotations.

Frederick Chamberlin, *The Private Character of Queen Elizabeth.* New York: Dodd Mead, 1922. A very unusual book that examines Elizabeth's medical condition and thoroughly delves into various charges against her, such as her supposed love affairs with Robert Dudley and Thomas Seymour.

Mary Hill Cole, *The Portable Queen: Elizabeth I and the Politics of Ceremony.* Amherst: University of Massachusetts Press, 1999. Thorough research is evident in this extremely detailed account of the famous progresses of Elizabeth I.

A.H. Dodd, *Elizabethan England.* New York: G.P. Putnam's Sons, 1973. A well-illustrated look at the various aspects of life and society in Elizabethan England.

Ian Dunlop, *Palaces and Progresses of Elizabeth I.* New York: Taplinger, 1970. This book provides an excellent description of Elizabeth's principal residences and lively accounts of her visits to the homes of some of her most well known subjects.

Ralph Dutton, *English Court Life from Henry VII to George II.* London: B.T. Batsford, 1963. This work traces the evolution of life and customs in England's royal court through almost three centuries of rulers.

Carolly Erickson, *The First Elizabeth.* New York: Summit, 1983. The author's expertise in medieval history is evident in this scholarly yet entertaining biography of Elizabeth. Particularly helpful for researchers is the exhaustive index.

Alan Glover, ed., *Gloriana's Glass.* London: Nonesuch, 1953. Interesting collection of contemporary documents, including descriptions of Elizabeth's court and poetry written about and by the queen.

Robert Gray, *A History of London.* New York: Taplinger, 1979. This book traces London from its beginnings as a Roman settlement through the 1970s, with attention to physical growth and social and political developments.

Lisa Hopkins, *Queen Elizabeth I and Her Court.* London: Vision, 1990. An excellent account that blends biographical information on Elizabeth with details of both the public face and inner workings of her court.

Joel Hurstfield and Alan G.R. Smith, eds., *Elizabethan People: State and Society.* New York: St. Martin's, 1972. A wonderful collection of excerpts from letters, speeches, acts of Parliament, and many other documents organized by topic and presenting a good picture of Elizabethan life.

Elizabeth Jenkins, *Elizabeth the Great.* New York: Capricorn, 1958. An outstanding biography of Elizabeth I; the examination of her personal life is particularly revealing.

Mary M. Luke, *Gloriana: The Years of Elizabeth I.* New York: Coward, McCann & Geoghegan, 1973. This book is the third in a series that also includes works on Catherine of Aragon and Elizabeth I's early life. This book concentrates on the queen's life after she ascended to the throne.

Garrett Mattingly, *The Armada.* Boston: Houghton Mifflin, 1959. A highly informative account, not only of the defeat of the Spanish Armada but also of all the political intrigue in Europe that led up to the events of 1588.

Christopher Morris, *The Tudors.* Glasgow: Fontana Collins, 1966. This source is more a study of the personalities of the Tudor kings and queens than a history of their reigns. It offers an excellent look at Elizabeth as the woman behind the mask of royalty.

Rachel and Allen Percival, *The Court of Elizabeth the First.* London: Stainer and Bell, 1976. A very interesting treatment of life in the court of Queen Elizabeth I, especially the inclusion of poetry and music.

Roger Pringle, ed., *Portrait of Elizabeth I.* Totowa, NJ: Barnes and Noble, 1980. Elizabeth's life and reign are examined through contemporary documents and literary works.

Alfred L. Rowse, *The Elizabethan Renaissance: The Cultural Achievement.* New York: Charles Scribner's Sons, 1972. This work is the fourth in the author's series on the England of Elizabeth; this one deals with art, literature, science, and philosophy.

———, *The Elizabethan Renaissance: The Life of the Society.* New York: Charles Scribner's Sons, 1971. This is the third of Rowse's four volumes on the Elizabethan era; this one deals principally with social life, including the court, social classes, and leisure activities.

———, *The England of Elizabeth.* Madison: University of Wisconsin Press, 1978. The first in a series of four books on the Elizabethan era by one of the most prominent scholars in the field. This volume deals mostly with commerce, government, and religion.

———, *The Expansion of Elizabethan England.* New York: St. Martin's, 1995. This volume in the author's series deals not only with overseas expansion but also with relations with Wales, Scotland, and Ireland.

Alfred L. Rowse and George B. Harrison, *Queen Elizabeth and Her Subjects.* Freeport, NY: Books for Libraries, 1935. A good examination of the reign of Elizabeth I, especially in its assessment of the spirit and accomplishments of the time and how it paved the way for future greatness.

Edith Sitwell, *The Queens and the Hive*. Boston: Little, Brown, 1962. This well-known poet is equally impressive in this lengthy yet highly readable account of the lives and reigns of Mary I and Elizabeth I of England and Mary, Queen of Scots.

Lacey Baldwin Smith, *The Elizabethan World*. Boston: Houghton Mifflin, 1967. A comprehensive look not only at Elizabethan England but also at the rest of Europe and the world beyond.

———, *The Horizon Book of the Elizabethan World*, ed. Norman Kotler. New York: American Heritage, 1967. The same text as the author's *Elizabethan World* but lavishly illustrated, it contains sections of contemporary works and quotations illustrating various aspects of the society.

John Southworth, *Fools and Jesters at the English Court*. Thrupp, England: Sutton, 1998. A fascinating account of the history of the court jesters throughout English history.

Milton Waldman, *Rod of Iron*. Boston: Houghton Mifflin, 1941. An interesting study of the ways in which power was wielded by English rulers in the sixteenth and first half of the seventeenth centuries. Particular attention is paid to Henry VIII, Elizabeth I, and Oliver Cromwell.

Susan Watkins, *In Public and Private: Elizabeth I and Her World*. New York: Thames and Hudson, 1998. An entertaining and well-illustrated biography of Elizabeth that includes not only the momentous political and religious events of the time but also the inner workings of the queen's household.

Violet Wilson, *Queen Elizabeth's Maids of Honour*. London: John Lane, 1922. The author's quaint style makes this account of the lives, loves, and troubles of Elizabeth's maids all the more enjoyable.

Internet Sources

Duncan Harrington, trans. "Two Entries from the Register of Archbishop John Whitgift, Lambeth Palace Library," Crandall Family Association, 2001. www.cfa.net/cfa/lambeth2.html.

J.J. O'Connor and E.F. Robertson, "John Dee," Turnbull www.server, August 2002. http://turnbull.mcs.st-and.ac.uk/~history/Mathematicians/Dee.html.

Sir Francis Bacon's New Advancement of Learning, "Quotes of Francis Bacon," www.sirbacon.org/links/baconquotes.html.

Index

Picture Credits

Cover Image: AKG Images
© Archivo Iconografico, S.A./CORBIS, (timeline), 14, 93
Art Resource, NY, (timeline)
© Bettmann/CORBIS, 72
Bildarchiv Preussischer Kulturbesitz/ Art Resource, NY, (timeline)
Bridgeman Art Library, 19, 21, 28, 32, 38, 49, 55, 60, 65, 66, 67, 70, 77, 88
Erich Lessing/Art Resource, NY, 73, 90
© Fine Art Photographic Library/CORBIS, (timeline), 11
© Francis G. Mayer/CORBIS, (timeline), 14
Giraudon/Art Resource, NY, 52
© Gustavo Tomsich/CORBIS, (timeline)
HIP/Art Resource, NY, 36, 51, 78
Hulton Archive/Getty Images, 57
© Joel W. Rogers/CORBIS, (timeline), 83
Library of Congress, (timeline)
Mary Evans Picture Library, 58
© Michael Nicholson/CORBIS, 17
North Wind Picture Archives, 42, 46, 62
Photodisc, (timeline), 31
© Stapleton Collection/CORBIS, 24, 85
Steve Zmina, 35, 41, 86
The Art Archive, 27
Time Life Pictures/Getty Images, 75
Victoria & Albert Museum, London/Art Resource, NY, 87

About the Author

William W. Lace is a native of Fort Worth, Texas, where he is executive assistant to the chancellor at Tarrant County College. He holds a bachelor's degree from Texas Christian University, a master's degree from East Texas State University, and a doctorate from the University of North Texas. Prior to joining Tarrant County College he was director of the News Service at the University of Texas at Arlington and a writer and columnist for the *Fort Worth Star-Telegram.* He has written more than twenty-five books for Lucent, one of which—*The Death Camps*—was selected by the New York Public Library for its 1999 Recommended Teenage Reading List. He and his wife, Laura, a retired school librarian, live in Arlington, Texas, and have two children and three grandchildren.